MOROCCO IN THE 21st CENTURY

Guy Arnold

NORTH SOUTH BOOKS

Copyright @ 2009 by North-South Books

Published by North-South Books in 2009

London

North-South Publications

10 Beaufort Court, Admirals Way, London E14 9XL, United Kingdom

Email: northsouthbooks@ aol.com

Catalogue record of this book is available from the British library

ISBN 978-0-9563070-2-6

Cover Photo: Linh/MAP

Printed in the United Kingdom

CONTENTS

Map of Morocco 05

Facts and figures about Morocco 06

Key Events in Morocco's History 08

Introduction 17

Chapter one: Brief Overview 19

Chapter two: The Royal Legacy 25

Chapter three: King Mohammed VI 33

- Moudawana.. 35

Chapter four: Politics and Government 41

- Parliament 41

- System of Government 44

Chapter five: Foreign Policy 49

- European Union 49

- France 51

- Spain 54

- The United States of America 58

- Arab World 60

- Maghreb.. 60

- Middle East Peace 63

- Africa 65

- Moroccan Diaspora 68

Chapter six: The Question of Western Sahara 71

Chapter seven: National Human Development Initiative (INDH) ... 81

Chapter eight: Human Rights 85

Chapter nine: Islam and Terrorism 95

CONTENTS

Chapter ten: Media and Freedom of Expression 103

Chapter eleven: Economic Overview 111

Chapter twelve: Trade, Industry and Agriculture 117

-Tanger-Med Port... 118

- Phosphates... 124

- Agriculture.. 127

Chapter thirteen: Tourism 133

Chapter fourteen: Problems and Prospects 139

Appendix 151

Government Ministers and Websites 162

Trade Unions... 165

Bilateral Treaties... 166

Useful Links... 167

Regions, Prefectures and Provinces 168

Consultative Councils... 170

Public Offices... 170

Financial and Professional Institutions....................... 171

International Organisations..................................... 174

Media Institutions.. 175

Trade Associations and Federations............................ 186

Foreign Embassies in Morocco 197

United Nations Representations................................. 217

African Institutions... 218

International Foundations....................................... 219

FACTS AND FIGURES ABOUT MOROCCO

People

Nationality:	Noun and adjective Moroccan(s)
Population:	34,343,220 (July 2008 est.)
Annual growth:	1.505% (2008 est.)
Birth rate:	21.31 births/1,000 population (2008 est.)
Death rate:	5.49 deaths/1,000 population (2008 est.)
Ethnic groups:	Arab-Berber 99%
Religions:	Muslim 99.99%, Jewish population estimated at 5,000 people, Christian population estimated at about 1,000
Languages:	Arabic (official), three Berber dialects (Tamazight, Tashalhit, Tarifit); Hassania in the Sahara, French used mostly as the language of business
Education:	Years compulsory 7. Literacy (definition-age 15 and over can read and write), total population 52.3% male; 65.7% female; 39.6% (2004 census)
Health:	Infant mortality rate (2008 est.), 38.22/1,000. Life expectancy at birth (2008 est.), 71.52 years, total population; 69.16 yrs. male; 74 yrs. female.
Work force:	11.5 million (2008 est.)
Unemployment:	9.9% (2008 est.)

Government

Type:	Constitutional monarchy
Constitution:	March 1972, revised 1980, 1992, and 1996 (creating a bicameral legislature)
Independence:	March 2, 1956
Branches:	Executive--King (head of state), Prime Minister (head of government). Legislative, Bicameral Parliament. Judicial, Supreme Court

Major political parties:
Istiqlal (Independence) Party (PI), Party of Justice and Development (PJD), Socialist Union of Popular Forces (USFP), National Rally of Independents (RNI), Popular Movement (MP), Constitutional Union Party (UC), Party of Progress and Socialism (PPS) and Pary of Modernity and Authenticity (PAM)
Suffrage: Universal starting at 18 years of age

Traditional Allegiance Ceremony

KEY EVENTS IN THE HISTORY OF MOROCCO

Man was already roaming along the Atlantic shoreline, as far back as 800,000 BC, as is evidenced by artefacts unearthed in Casablanca – the most ancient finds ever discovered in North Africa. Towards 5000 BC, settlers from the Near East co-existed and intermixed with the indigenous inhabitants of Morocco. These newcomers were the ancestors of the Berbers, their numbers further increased and mixed with other Mediterranean people.

Date	Event
642	The Arab incursion in North-West Africa. Only nine years after the death of the prophet Muhammad
683-732	Dissemination of Islam in Morocco under Okba Ibn Nafi and Tarik Ibn Ziad's conquest of Gibraltar and Spain
788	Arrival of Moulay Idriss I in Morocco, a descendent of the Prophet, and the emergence of the Idrissides' (788-823) dynasty and the establishment of the Islamic state
808	reign of Idriss II (808-823)
808	Founding of the city of Fez
1055-1147	Reign of the Almoravides dynasty
1070	Founding of the city of Marrrakech
1130-1268	Reign of the Almohads dynasty
1269-1465	Reign of the Merinides dynasty
1466-1549	Reign of the Wattasids dynasty
1549-1654	Reign of the Saadians dynasty
1578	Oued Al Makhazine (the Balltle of the Thre Kings)
1664-1672	Reign of Moulay Rachid
1672-1727	Reign of Moulay Ismaïl, founder of the city of Meknès
1729-1757	Reign of Moulay Abdellah
1757-1790	Reign of Sidi Mohammed Ben Abdellah
1790-1792	Reign of Moulay Yazid
1792-1822	Reign of Moulay Soulaiman
1822-1859	Reign of Moulay Abderrahman. Start of the French occupation of Algeria (1830): Morocco

	strongly supported the Algerian resistance movement led by Emir Abdelkader
1859-1873	Reign of Mohammed IV
1873-1894	Reign of Moulay Hassan I
1884	Spain imposed an illegal and unilateral "protectorate" on the territory of Rio de Oro (Dakhla).
1887	Sultan Hassan I names Sheikh Ma El-Ainin his deputy in the Sahara
1894-1908	Reign of Moulay Abdelaziz. During this period (in 1904) the Moroccan Sahara was shared out by secret treaty between France and Spain; the Algeciras Accord was signed in 1906 and Casablanca was attacked by the French in 1907
1902	Ma El Ainin settles in Smara
1908-1912	Reign of Moulay Abdelhafid. The Protectorate Treaty dividing Morocco into French, Spanish and international zones of influence was signed on 30 March 1912
1912-1956	French and Spanish protectorate in Morocco
1912-1927	Reign of Moulay Youssef. Resistance to French and Spanish occupation (Rif war)
18 Nov 1927	Enthronement of HM Mohammed V at the age of 18
11 Jan 1944	Presentation of the Independence Manifesto to the representative of the French government in Morocco
9 Apr 1947	Trip by King Mohammed V to Tangier where he delivered a speech marking the revival of resistance to foreign occupation
20 Aug 1953	Exile of King Mohammed V and his family to Madagascar
16 Nov 1955	Return from exile of King Mohammed V
2 Mar 1956	Signing of the 'Celle-Saint Cloud' agreements recognising the independence of the Kingdom of Morocco
7 Apr 1956	Agreement with Spain ending the Spanish protectorate over the Moroccan northern provinces
1956	Within a month of Morocco's independence, anti-Spanish demonstrations occurred in Ifni and the months of June and July 1956 marked the start of Morocco's liberation army

	activity within Western Sahara.
22 Apr 1956	Morocco becomes a member of the United Nations Organisation
1957	Moroccan army of liberation staged its first attack on Spanish garrisons in Western Sahara
1958	A joint Franco-Spanish military counter-insurgency campaign (Operation Ouragan or Ecouvillion) drove thousands of Sahrawis to flee into Morocco
1958	Morocco and Spain signed the Cintra agreement (1 April) by which the province of Tarfaya was handed over to Morocco
3 Mar 1961	Enthronement of HM King Hassan II (1961-1999)
1963	First elections under King Hassan II
1962	Morocco addressed an official request to the UN Decolonisation Committee in June calling on Spain to enter into negotiations over handing over the occupied territories.
1964	The UN called on Spain to apply UN 1960 Declaration on the occupied territories of Ifni and Western Sahara.
1965	Spanish African territories were to figure on the UN General Assembly agenda for the first time.
1965	UN Resolution 2072 of 16/12/1965 called on Spain to enter into negotiations with Morocco over Western Sahara and Sidi Ifni.
4 Jan 1969	Treaty of Fez and recovery of the city of Sidi Ifni, formerly under Spanish rule
1972	Third Constitution approved by popular referendum. The new Constitution kept King Hassan's powers intact while enlarging from one-third to two-thirds the number of directly elected parliamentary representatives
1974	Madrid announced the holding of a referendum in 1975 for integration with Spain or independence. Morocco objected for being ruled out of the process.
1974	Morocco called on the UN General Assembly to refer the issue to the International Court of Justice (ICJ) in The Hague.

1974	Algerian President Houari Boumedienne declared his solemn support for Morocco's claims over Western Sahara at the Arab Summit in Rabat.
1975	Spain announced officially it would not be bound by the ICJ verdict
1975	The ICJ decided that there existed historical and legal ties of allegiance between the Sultan of Morocco and tribes in Western Sahara.
1975	Upon Spain's refusal to enter into negotiations with Morocco to hand over the disputed territory, King Hassan II decided to launch the Green March on 6 November with 350,000 volunteers marching into the Western Sahara
1975	The Madrid Accord on 14 November put an end to Spain's occupation of Western Sahara and the agreement was reached in accordance with article 33 of the UN Charter and Security Council resolution 380. The agreement was also approved by the "Jema'a", an assembly of notables representing all tribes in the territory.
1976	Spain's formal withdrawal from the territory. Polisario launched attacks on Moroccan troops from southern Algeria with Libya and Algeria as the main backers. The Sahrawi Arab Democratic Republic (SADR) was also proclaimed in Algeria (27 February).
1976	A Moroccan-Algerian armed confrontation took place in Amghala on 19 January and some 130 Algerian soldiers were captured and later freed.
1976	The Algerian authorities deported some 45.000 Moroccans who were living in Algeria legally and married to Algerians. Families were torn apart by such politically motivated decision. Morocco never reacted to such human tragedy of unprecedented scale.
Aug 1979	The Algiers Accord and Moroccan conquest of the rest of the Western Sahara
1981	King Hassan II announced a referendum in Western Sahara at the OAU Summit in Nairobi.
1982	The Secretary General of the Organisation of African Unity (OAU), Edem Kodjo, made the unilateral

	decision to admit "SADR" as a member state without prior consultation with the Implementation Committee or the Chairman of the OAU, President Arap Moi of Kenya. The decision resulted in the organisation being divided between "moderates" and "progressive" states.
1984	Morocco decided to withdraw from the OUA following the violation of article 4, 27 and 28 of the OAU Charter.
1984	The Western Saharan dispute was moved to the UN.
1988	A UN Peace plan was accepted by all conflicting parties in the Sahara issue
17 Feb 1989	Signing of the treaty establishing the Arab Maghreb Union (UMA) in Marrakech
1990	A Settlement Plan was endorsed by the Security Council in June.
1991	A UN brokered cease-fire came into force between the conflicting parties in Western Sahara on 6 September 1991. A UN referendum was set up in the area "MINURSO". An identification process of eligible voters began to find out who was eligible to vote for integration with Morocco or independence. MINURSO was trusted with the task to compile a list of eligible voters who can vote in the referendum.
1991	UN-sponsored ceasefire in Western Sahara
4 Sep 1992	Referendum to amend the 1972 Constitution
16 Oct1992	Local elections
29 Aug 1993	Inauguration of the Hassan II Mosque, Casablanca 25 June
17 Sep 1993	General elections
27 May 1995	King Hassan II meets Yasser Arafat and Shimon Peres in an attempt to broker peace between Palestinians and Israelis
1995	The Idendification process broke down
1996	On the advice of the UN Secretary-General, the Security Council voted on 29 May 1996 to suspend the identification process.
13 Sep 1996	Adoption by referendum of the new draft bicameral constitution, with a House of Representatives elected

	via direst universal suffrage, and a second House of Counsellors elected via indirect suffrage
1997	The UN Secretary-General, Kofi Annan, appointed former US Secretary of State, James Baker, to be his Personal Envoy with a remit to assess the feasibility of the UN Settlement Plan.
1997	A series of talks led to the Houston Agreement in September. This in turn led to the resumption, in December 1997, of voter identification.
2 Apr 1997	Promulgation of the Regional Law and the Laws on the Statutes of the Chambers of Agriculture, Chambers of Commerce and Industry and Services, Chambers of Handicraft and Maritime Chambers
1 May 1997	Promulgation of the Royal Decree setting up an electoral commission and regional commissions for the supervision of the elections
13 June 1997	Local elections held in Morocco: 102,179 candidates to fill the 24,253 seats in the 1547 urban and rural communes
15 Jul 1997	Election pf provincial and prefectoral assemblies
25 Jul 1997	Election of professional chambers
24 Oct 1997	Election of regional counsellors
14 Nov 1997	Organisation of general elections to choose 325 MPs to sit in the House of the Representatives
5 Dec 1997	Election via indirect suffrage of the 270 members of the House of Counsellors
4 Feb 1998	King Hassan II asks Abderrahmane Youssoufi, First Secretary of the USFP, to form a new government
14 Mar 1998	King Hassan II meets the new government in the Throne Room
23 Jul 1999	Death of King Hassan II and ceremony of allegiance of Crown Prince Sidi Mohammed
2000	The UN Secretary General and his Personal Envoy, James Baker, concluded that the Settlement plan can not be implemented and that another approach must be sought because of disputes over the eligibility of voters. People of the same tribe and sometimes the same

family were excluded from voting so thousands appealed and the identification process was halted as it would take years for it to be completed partly because of the inhabitants were mostly nomads of no fixed abode. The UN opted for another approach and proposed a Framework agreement that would allow the Sahrawis the right to elect their own executive and legislative bodies, under Moroccan sovereignty, and have exclusive competence over a number of areas namely: local government administration, territorial budget and tax law enforcement, internal security, social welfare, culture, education, commerce, transportation, agriculture, mining, industry, fisheries, environmental policy, housing and urban development, water and electricity and other basic infrastructure. James Baker "reiterated that there were many ways to achieve self-determination". Security Council Resolution 1309 of 25 July 2000, Called for an acceptable political solution.

2001	The Baker framework agreement was endorsed by the UN Security Council resolution 1359. Morocco accepted the proposal but Algeria and the Polisario "expressed strong reservations" to the draft framework agreement
2001	The Algerian president, Abdelaziz Bouteflika, proposed, instead, another option in November that of the partition of the territory.
2002	A UN Secretary General report published on 19 February included four alternative solutions to the problem namely the resumption of the UN Settlement Plan, James Baker to revise the Framework Agreement, the partition of the territory or the termination of MINURSO by the UN Security Council.
May 2003	The UN Secretary General's four alternative solutions were the resumption of the UN settlement Plan,

	James Baker to revise the Framework Agreement, the partition of the territory or the termination of MINURSO by the UN Security Council.
2005	Peter Van Walsum was appointed as the UN Secretary General Personal Envoy for the Western Sahara.
2006	After the UN-brokered cease-fire on 6 September 1991, it took Algeria and the Polisario fifteen years to release hundreds of prisoners of war some of whom had spent over twenty five years in holes in the ground covered with corrugated iron and who were used as slave labour in the Tindouf camps, in South-West Algeria. Their release was finally secured thanks to the intervention of American senators Richard Lugar and John McCain.
2007	Prior to the adoption of Resolution 1754 and the start of the ongoing UN-sponsored negotiations, Morocco had submitted a proposal to grant full autonomy to the Saharan region within the framework of the Kingdom's sovereignty and territorial integrity.
Apr 2007	Morocco responded favourably to the UN Security Council resolution 1754 asking the conflicting parties to negotiate without preconditions under UN auspices, the Manhasset h meetings took place in search for a political solution.
30 Jul 2007	In a speech to mark the 8th anniversary of his enthronement, King Mohammed VI stated that Morocco was ready to negotiate on the basis of a consensual autonomy solution conceived within the framework of the kingdom's sovereignty.
7 Sep 2007	General elections for the chamber of representative. New government headed by Prime Minister Abbas al-Fassi, leader of the Istiqlal party that won most seats.
2007	The UN-sponsored talks took place in Manhasset (Greentree Estate) near New York, on 18-19 June and 10-11 August 2007 and 7-8 January and 16-18 March 2008. The first rounds of negotiations served as an icebreaker after years of hostility between the conflicting parties who reiterated their

	willingnessto cooperate with the UN to break the stalemate.
Apr 2008	In his assessment of the situation on the ground, Peter van Walsum, the United Nations Secretary General's special envoy and mediator in talks on Western Sahara declared before the UN Security Council that, "an independent Western Sahara was not a realistic proposition". He also pointed out that the organisation of a referendum was "unworkable".
2008	UN Security Council resolution 1813 (30 April 2008) called on "the parties to continue to show political will and work in an atmosphere propitious for dialogue in order to enter into a more intensive and substantive phase of negotiations".
2009	The American diplomat, Christopher Ross, was appointed UN Secretary General's Personal Envoy for Western Sahara to help broker a lasting and acceptable political solution.
12 Jun 2009	Local elections. The Authenticity and Modernity Party (PAM) secured 21.7% of the 27,795 seats and voters turn out reached 52.4%. PAM, founded in mid 2008, emerged as Morocco's largest opposition party.

INRODUCTION

Morocco is one of a few countries in the world that can trace their nationhood existence as far back as the 7th century and claim a unique perspective on global events.

Due to its strategic position on the narrow Strait of Gibraltar that links the Mediterranean with the Atlantic, Morocco has always been a focal point of international, Arab, Islamic and African interest. Important too, is the role played by the centuries-old royal Alawite dynasty of which King Mohammed VI is the twenty- second sovereign.

The country's natural defences, represented by the Atlas mountain chains, the Sahara, the Mediterranean and the Atlantic Ocean, provide it with a unique strategic position and a distinctive culture and civilisation.

Morocco, as a bridge between Africa and Europe and a link between the West and the Arab and Muslim World, is one of the oldest monarchies in the world (second to Japan), having been founded some 12 centuries ago.

The King embodies both the spiritual and temporal authority which provides him with the title of "Commander of the Faithful" (Amir Al Muminin).

Throughout history, Islam in Morocco has woven indelible ties of tolerance with the other revealed religions; Christianity and Judaism. Moderate Sunni Islam in Morocco remains an important element in the fabrics of society.

Morocco is also confronted by the surge of political Islam sweeping the Muslim world but Moroccans have espoused Sunni Islam and pride themselves on their tolerant interpretation of religion and what has come to be known as "the Moroccan exception". The King is faced with the daunting challenge to preserve and maintain this crucial balance as a western-oriented Muslim nation and a tolerant society and at the same time must continue to articulate the vision of a democratic and modern Morocco.

During the first decade of the 21st century, Morocco has gone through an interesting and important transitional phase of its existence marked by bold initiatives and new developments that will transform the country from traditional conservatism to a modern and forward looking one.

Moroccans are deeply aware of their identity as descendents of the great Muslim empires that ruled Andalusia and much of North Africa in the Middle Ages. The deep-seated attachement to its Arab and African identity explains the kingdom's natural solidarity towards the African continent and the Arab world.

Moroccans regard the institution of the monarchy as guarantor of the country's unity, security, ethnic homogeneity, political and social stability and territorial integrity. The existence of a constitutional monarchy has not impeded the introduction of modern political, economic and social reforms.

King Mohammed VI, affectionately referred to as "M6", has been on the move since his advent on the throne in 1999 touring every corner of the Kingdom and initiating numerous social, economic and infrastructural projects. Over the past decade, he embarked on a number of significant ventures to eradicate poverty, illiteracy, corruption and social injustice as well as putting an end to violations of human rights and inequality of the sexes. He has made important changes to reform the economy and the media landscape, to adopt macroeconomic framework, to promote foreign investment and social development, to improve infrastructure and lay a solid foundation for strong and enduring growth in order to integrate his country into the global financial and economic environment. He has pursued his father's pro-Western policies and upgraded relations with the European Union to a strategic partnership.

There is an increasing hunger among the younger generation of Moroccans for the good things of modern times, as flaunted daily by global television channels and the internet. Morocco is an ancient country engaged in the transition to modernity and heading for the global economic village.

Despite real progress in the last ten years, problems typical of an emerging market continue to pose serious challenges for the King, the government and the people of Morocco.

This book aims to provide an overall view of King Mohammed VI's decade at the helm of this old nation dating back to the seventh century and what reforms, changes and progress have taken place in tackling the political, social and economic challenges facing his country as well as future prospects.

CHAPTER ONE: BRIEF OVERVIEW

Situated at the western extremity of North Africa with coastlines on both the Mediterranean and the Atlantic, Morocco is strategically placed in relation to Sub-Saharan Africa, the Maghreb, the Arab world and Europe. It has a long historical connection with Spain, a shorter if intense relationship with France, and has established closer relations with the European Union (EU) and the United States. Morocco covers 710.850 square kilometres of territory including the spectacular scenery of the Rif and the High Atlas mountains as well as the dry Anti-Atlas Mountains in the centre and the Sahara Desert in the south. Its Mediterranean and Atlantic coastline extends to over 3,500 kilometres and the fertile coastal plains are the country's agricultural heartland and the most heavily populated region. Morocco is 14 Km away from Europe and separated from Spain by the Straits of Gibraltar.

Its main languages are Arabic (official), Berber, French and Spanish. The country possesses a range of natural resources that include phosphates, iron ore, manganese, zinc, lead, salt, cobalt and silver although its huge phosphates resources are by far the most important to the economy. Morocco is the world's leading exporter of phosphates (the basis for fertiliser) and controls 25 per cent of the world market.

Arabised Berbers (the original inhabitants) are the main linguistic group while less assimilated Berbers account for a third of the population and many Moroccans speak both Arabic and Berber. Since independence in 1956, the French and Spanish minorities have become much smaller though they remain important. Other minorities are the Bedouin of the desert, blacks and Jews. This racial and multicultural mix gives the Moroccan population a unique character of its own although there is a divide between the coastal regions where European and Arab cultures mix and the interior or south which is dominated by the Berbers and Bedouin. There was a substantial Sephardic Jewish population in Morocco, whose roots in the country go back more than 2000 years, but following the 1967 Israeli-Arab war, many Jews left for Israel, France and Canada and their numbers have been reduced to little about 10,000. Morocco has consistently shown tolerance to this minority and this has been especially important in recent years when Jews would not have received such treatment in most other Arab countries. About 32 per cent of Morocco's population is aged 15 years or younger, while migration from the poor rural areas to the towns has transformed the country into an urban dominated one with 59 per cent of the people living in the towns. This movement to the towns has created major problems including a high level of unemployment that exceeds 10 per cent. Migration from the countryside to the towns is a problem throughout Africa and in Morocco the expectation of finding jobs in the urban centres far outweighs any work availability. About eight million Moroccans speak Berber and King Mohammed VI has made considerable efforts to make his Berber subjects less inclined to feel discriminated against. In 2001, the King established a Royal Institute for the Preservation of Berber Language and Culture. This initiative led to Berber language news programmes and the introduction of Berber language classes in 2003, a Television Channel in 2009 and even the ministry of interior announced that *Caids* (local officials) would have to learn Berber to officiate in Berber dominated areas.

French is widely spoken by the older generation and educated classes and is the language of business, science and education. Spanish is spoken in the northwest of the country. English and German are becoming more common in business, banking and the main tourist areas. The overwhelming majority of Moroccans are Sunni Muslims belonging to the Malikite creed, one of the four orthodox creeds in Islam, while the King is also the "Commander of the Faithful" and as such the country's supreme religious authority. Sufism is common and Morocco has many Sufi holy places and festivals.

Romans, Visigoths, Vandals, Byzantine Greeks and Phoenicians ruled successively in early years of Moroccan history. Arab forces began occupying Morocco in the seventh century A.D., bringing their civilisation and Islam. The Alawite dynasty, which has ruled Morocco since 1666, claims descent from the Prophet Muhammad.

Morocco is an old nation. It has geographical unity, long historical continuity and cultural traditions and its history can be traced back for 3,000 years. Pride in its past is a source of strength especially at a time of rapid change and development as Morocco seeks to find its place in a highly competitive world. It is the only nation of North Africa that did not come under Ottoman rule for the advancing Turks were halted at the Moroccan frontier. The sovereignty of Moroccan Sultans once reached as far south as Senegal and this historical fact is never forgotten. The present royal dynasty dates from 1666.

Morocco retained its independence into the 20th century until, in European terms, there were to be two Moroccan "crises" in 1905-06 and 1911 which acted as the prelude to France obtaining control of Morocco as one of the final acts in the European Scramble for Africa. In 1904 France concluded a secret treaty with Spain to partition Morocco. Germany, however, was insisting upon an open door policy in the region and to emphasise this policy on 31 March 1905 the German Kaiser, Wilhelm II, visited Tangier on his yacht and announced that he supported Morocco's independence and integrity. He sparked an immediate crisis between the four leading European powers – Britain, France, Germany and Spain. The crisis was resolved early in 1906 at the Algeciras Conference at which German and other national economic "rights" in Morocco were upheld while France and Spain were "entrusted" with policing Morocco. Then in February 1908 another Franco-German agreement reaffirmed Morocco's independence while recognising France's "special political interests" in the country and, more generally, Germany's economic interests in North Africa. The second Moroccan crisis erupted in 1911 when Germany sent a gunboat, the *Panther,* to Agadir on 1 July, to protect German interests during a local disturbance but in reality to exert political pressure upon France. The "Agadir Incident" led to talk of war but international mediation led to a convention of 4 November 1911, which gave France rights to establish a protectorate over Morocco. The Treaty of Fez (1912) made Morocco a protectorate of France. By the same treaty, Spain assumed the role of protecting power over the northern and southern (Saharan) zones of the country. The great powers granted Tangier and its environs a special status and it became an international city in 1923. The French protectorat only lasted 44 years until 1956 when Morocco gained its independence from France and Spain. Morocco is the only African country to have been under two colonial powers while Tangier was administered by an international commission. It remained an international zone until 1956, when it was integrated with the independent kingdom of Morocco.

Morocco is a constitutional monarchy and the constitution vests supreme executive power in the hereditary monarch and there is a parliamentary system of government. In recent years, under Mohammed VI there has been a degree of political liberalisation and decentralisation although the King retains ultimate authority and has direct control over the ministries of the Interior, Foreign Affairs, Religious Affairs and Justice, as well as the military. The bicameral parliament is divided into two chambers. The lower house, the House of Representatives, comprises 325 seats and is elected every five years by universal suffrage. All Moroccans over the age of 18 can vote. The upper house, the Chamber of Counsellors, comprises 270 seats and is elected by local councils, professional organisations and trade unions for nine-year non-consecutive terms with one third taking their seats every three years. The most important political parties are the centre-left *Union Socialiste des Forces Populaires (USFP);* the centre-right *Istiqlal* party; the mainstream Islamic *Parti de la Justice et du Developpement (PJD)*; and the centre-right Popular Movement (MP). Following the 2007 elections, The *Istiqlal* won the most seats but not a clear majority so the Prime Minister Abbas el Fassi, leader of the *Istiqlal,* was invited by the King to form a coalition government.

Moroccans wish to modernise, to be Muslim but also to see Islamic reforms and a greater say in government by the political parties although the position of the monarch as both King and Commander of the Faithful is widely accepted. The country is undergoing profound social changes and is now largely a money-based economy. The huge growth of urban Morocco has seen a changing elite which both relies upon traditional aspects of Moroccan culture while also adopting European lifestyles. Crucial for the future will be the attitudes of the country's youth who form nearly a third of the population. Three problems act as a background to the progress that has been achieved in recent years: these are illiteracy (40 per cent of the population), unemployment (11 per cent) and poverty.

MONARCHS OF MOROCCO SINCE INDEPENDENCE

King Mohammed V   *King Hassan II*

Princess Lalla Salma with King Mohammed VI and Crown Prince Moulay Hassan

King Mohammed VI with his wife Princess Lalla Salma and Prince Moulay Hassan

CHAPTER TWO: THE ROYAL LEGACY

Morocco won independence from France in 1956 and was ruled for the rest of the century by Kings Mohammed V (1927-1961) and Hassan II (1961-1999). King Mohammed V earned great prestige for his role in achieving independence from France and though he pursued conservative policies at home he blunted criticism by a militant foreign policy that was exactly suited to the general mood of nationalism sweeping through Africa at the time. During 1959 and 1960 he aligned himself with the revolutionary camp and presided at the January 1961 Casablanca summit of the "radical" states. At the time Mohammed V returned to Morocco from French exile in 1956, he was seen as the champion of the country's independence. This put him in a strong position to dominate the political process and allowed him to sideline the political parties that might have challenged his position. These included the Istiqlal (independence) party, which had led the struggle against France, and the leftwing *Union Nationale des Forces Populaires (UNFP)* that had split from Istiqlal to win Morocco's first post-independence elections. However, the King dismissed the UNFP cabinet and formed his own, also acting as prime minister. He then consolidated his power by rallying to his side the rural (conservative) notables and the security services. He was able to enshrine this monarchical system by capitalising on his popularity and charisma, as well as the general regard for the monarchy, which had a long history. Thus, the post-independence political system was established by Mohammed V and did not really change until the reforms introduced in the 1990s, during the last decade of King Hassan II's rule. The system allowed pluralism and economic liberalism at a time when Third World countries were opting for one party state political systems. Morocco allowed a variety of parties to be formed of all tendencies.

Five years after independence Mohammed V died during the course of an operation and was succeeded by his son, Hassan II, who had been deported by the French to Madagascar in exile with his father in 1953 and returned with him in 1956. Hassan claimed descent from the Prophet Mohammed and bore the titles "Commander of the Faithful" and "Allah's Deputy on Earth". He maintained an Islamic state but without extremism. All real power rested in his hands throughout his long reign and he remained an autocrat who saw that changes or reforms came from the top down. On coming to the throne, King Hassan inherited a poor country that was deeply in debt, a population many of whom were illiterate and a high level of unemployment. During his reign the population was to increase from 10 million to 30 million and this steady rise in population "swallowed" all the economic gains that were achieved. Unlike his father, Hassan pursued a moderate, largely neutral foreign policy, which earned for him some economic support from abroad. His first political reform in 1963 was to allow elections for a two-chamber legislature. However, he reserved for himself the right to appoint and dismiss ministers and to preside at cabinet meetings. Following the outbreak of riots in Casablanca in 1965 the king assumed direct rule under a state of emergency. Hassan II was to survive several coup attempts during his reign (1971 and 1972); their impact made him more authoritarian.

In 1975, King Hassan led the "Green March" of 350,000 unarmed Moroccans across the border into the Spanish colony of Western Sahara to register his country's claim to the territory as part of Morocco. However, this peaceful "victory" was the prelude to the long war with the Libyan and Algerian-backed Polisario and confrontation with the country's neighbour Algeria which has been supporting and arming the Polisario and wanting access to the Atlantic. In the course of the war, after setbacks, King Hassan adopted a wall strategy: huge sand walls and detector systems were constructed to deny the Polisario guerrillas access to the territory. He tried to promote the peace process in the Middle East and like his father protected the Jewish minority. He believed that the acceptance of the presence of Jews in Morocco would demonstrate that Arabs and Jews could live together peacefully. In 1986 he met Israel's then Prime Minister Shimon Peres. He established good relations with King Juan Carlos of Spain as well as good relations with the United States, which came to see Morocco as a firm African ally during the Cold War.

King Hassan erected a mausoleum to his Father Mohammed V in Rabat and it emerged as a monument to Islamic art. He then restored all the national, civic and court buildings and in the process restored the artisan class, many of whose traditional skills – in copper work, silver, leather, ceramics, woodwork and sculpted plaster – would otherwise have been lost. Thus he inspired a new phase of building in Morocco that became known as the Hassan II style. At the beginning of his reign there were an estimated 300 master craftsmen in the country but by the middle of his reign, as a result of this building programme, the number had risen to 30,000 and these craftsmen have subsequently been in demand for work throughout the Arab world.

In 1961, King Hassan inherited a system of direct monarchical rule with power concentrated in the hands of the king while there was only a weak, fragmented popular political system that might have opposed him. Over the next thirty years, Hassan II consolidated his position by undermining opposition and limiting independent political life by institutional manipulation, reliance upon client networks created by patronage and if necessary by manipulation. The 1962 constitution confirmed this royal position of control by giving the king powers to nominate or dismiss the prime minister and the cabinet at his discretion. It also empowered him to dissolve parliament and assume unlimited emergency powers. The constitution was to be revised in 1970, 1980, 1992 and 1996 but none of these revisions reduced the royal powers. The monarch's power is reinforced by the Muslim religion since the King of Morocco is considered to be a descendant of the Prophet and, as Amir al Mu-minim or Commander of the Faithful, is the supreme religious authority in the country, a fact that would be of huge importance to his successor when he embarked upon religious reforms. Hassan II used the traditional network of monarchical institutions known as the makhzen, a term denoting an elite of palace retainers, regional provincial administrators and military officers. In effect, the *makhzen* includes all people in the service of the monarchy and brings in others in receipt of royal patronage. This system made the king all-powerful. He permitted political parties to exist but played them off against each other or co-opted key political figures into the *makhzen* structure. He encouraged the rise of new political groups so as to divide and check the existing ones.

In the 1960s and 1970s, when there were considerable challenges to the king's authority, including two attempted coups in 1971 and 1972, the reactions of the government could be brutal. Hundreds of palace opponents were abducted and disappeared, dozens were imprisoned and sometimes tortured and anyone perceived to be an enemy of the regime risked becoming a victim. The majority of those affected by these repressive measures were leftists, revolutionaries or hard line

Islamists. Only in the 1990s did King Hassan embark upon reforms when he felt obliged to respond to the changed world climate that followed the end of the Cold War and growing Western insistence upon democracy. Further pressures upon the king followed a series of severe droughts that forced many rural people to move to the cities in search of work. The result was increased unemployment and social unrest, which in their turn led to an increase in support for hostile Islamist groups. Moreover, there was mounting international criticism of Morocco's human rights record. Reforms fell broadly into four categories: improved respect for human rights; a limited increase in the powers of parliament; enhanced opportunities for political participation by parties and civil society; and curbs on corruption though this last reform made little progress. Much of King Hassan's reforming effort was directed at improving human rights since these especially made headlines outside the country. He formed a Human Rights Council and later a Ministry for Human Rights. These reforms included the release of some political prisoners, a tightening of the laws governing preventive detention and demonstrations, the formation of a special committee to investigate forced disappearances and the ratification of a number of international human rights conventions. Even so, the reforms were limited in scope and, for example, thousands of political prisoners remained in jail. Shortly before he died, the King admitted that forced disappearances had taken place though he did not accept any state responsibility.

The revised 1996 constitution laid down that the king could veto bills that had been approved by parliament or amend them without the need to re-submit them to parliament as well as being able to issue laws directly, without any consultation with parliament. He involved all parties in decisions affecting the conduct of elections and following the elections to the two chambers in 1997 he did not ask the "palace" parties to form a government but instead asked Abderrahman El Youssoufi, leader of the USFP, to form the government. El Youssoufi was a long-term opponent of the monarchical regime who had twice been imprisoned and had spent fifteen years in exile. His government of national unity, however, had only a limited impact. An important factor that had influenced the king to open up the political system was the rise of Islamist extremism; he wanted to mobilise the secular political parties to oppose such extremism. What the King had done was create a system of alternance under which he brought in the two main opposition parties to assist in the fight against extremism while not surrendering any of his own powers. The King kept in his hands the appointment of ministers to three "sovereignty" ministries: the Interior, Foreign Affairs and Justice. At the same time the king had permitted an Islamist party to be formed, which could be used to check the power of the left. King Hassan II died on 23 July 1999.However, the reform process led to some significant changes in Morocco. Human rights conditions improved and there was at least a partial acknowledgement of former abuses. The taboo on discussing corruption was lifted and some economic reforms were initiated. King Hassan's strategy was to co-opt party leaders and pit the parties against each other to ensure that no party or group became strong enough to challenge his authority. An important stimulus to reform was the civil war that engulfed Algeria through the 1990s; a flexible system would more easily enable Morocco to avoid comparable extremism. The moves towards a more open society were relative, however, since thousands of political prisoners remained in jail. Under the constitutional amendments of 1992 and 1996 parliament was turned into a bicameral body whose lower chamber was elected by universal suffrage while the upper chamber was indirectly elected by trade unions, trade associations and various organizations. King Hassan allowed the Islamist organisation Al Isla wal Tajdid (Reform and Renewal) to participate in the 1997 elections. Later Al Isla wal Tajdid formed the *Parti de la Justice et Developpement (PJD)*. The rise of political Islam undoubtedly aided King Hassan's political reforms by persuading the old secular parties to join forces with the monarchy. Alternance was an ambiguous strategy but by bringing the opposition parties into government it signalled that the monarchy was open to the democratic process. Perhaps the most important of the King's reform strategies was that of encouraging civil society organisations to speak out, especially on the issue of corruption. This was the beginning of a lasting process in which human rights organisations made state abuses a matter of public discussion and women's organisations began to agitate and negotiate for reform of the Mudawana.

King Hassan's long reign has been described as one of enlightened authoritarian rule with all essential power concentrated in the hands of the king. Assisted by the creation of a modern bureaucracy, the king was not accountable to anyone and expected total obedience from ministers, governors, senators and magistrates: they enjoyed prerogatives but wielded little real power. They were called "khudama" – loyal servants to the throne rather than representing any political institutions that possessed their own authority. Moreover, the King's title Commander of the Faithful was no sinecure but meant that religious scholars and leaders who were supposed to represent the community in fact were beholden to the King and could not independently represent the interests of the communities they served. The King conferred many benefits upon his close allies and collaborators but in return expected loyalty and discretion: they could not attempt to become independent powers through the offices they held. Although Hassan II inaugurated an anti-corruption campaign no action was taken against senior officials who enriched themselves through corrupt practices. The King succeeded in projecting an international image of enlightenment, moderation and stability but at a social price that included some repression at home. And at the end of his long reign almost half the population was illiterate of whom 70 per cent were women, 19 per cent of Moroccans lived in poverty and over 20 per cent of the work force, including 100,000 university graduates, were unemployed. Most rural villages had no access to paved roads, running water or electricity and almost none had access to basic health care facilities. This legacy faced King Hassan's son who became King Mohammed VI after his father's death on 23 July 1999.

King Mohammed VI inaugurating Tangier-Med port

Photo: Linh/MAP

King Mohammed VI on the move

Photos: Linh/MA

مؤسسة محمد الخامس للتضامن

Linh/MAP

CHAPTER THREE: KING MOHAMMED VI

King Mohammed VI was born on 21 August 1963 and ascended the throne in July 1999. At the age of four his father King Hassan II enrolled him at the Koranic school in the Royal Palace. On 28 June 1973, Mohammed, then Crown Prince, obtained the primary education certificate and continued secondary studies at the royal College where he got his Baccalaureate in 1981. In 1985 he obtained his B.A. in law at the Rabat Mohammed V University and then carried out a research project on "the Arab-African Union and the Strategy of the Kingdom of Morocco in matters of International Relations". In 1987 he obtained a higher diploma in political sciences and in July 1988, he graduated with a Master's degree. In November 1988 he trained in Brussels under Jacques Delors, the President of the European Commission. In October 1993 he obtained his doctorate in law (PhD) from the French University of Nice Sophia Antipolis for his thesis on "EEC-Maghreb Relations". On 12 July 1994 Prince Mohammed was appointed coordinator of the Armed forces. King Hassan II, who referred to his son's education as a grooming for Kingship, died on 23 July 1999, and was succeeded by his eldest son, Crown Prince Sidi Mohammed as King Mohammed VI. Little was known about the new king, who was then aged 36. As Crown Prince he had remained in his father's shadow and though groomed for the succession, King Hassan had not put him in any politically responsible jobs so that Mohammed was able to come to the throne free of entanglements that would have committed him to particular courses of action. His father's attempt to protect him from any political commitment or responsibility meant that he could start his reign with a clean slate.

In his first speech to the nation, King Mohammed pledged to support the multiparty system, economic liberalisation, regional decentralisation, the rule of law and respect for human rights and individual liberties. He also reaffirmed his support for the principle of *alternance*. The accession of Mohammed VI in 1999 gave rise to considerable expectations that some far-reaching reforms would follow. The King projected a very different persona from that of his father, who had been distant, aloof and deeply conservative. He cast himself as a modern monarch who wanted to meet his subjects: the "King of the poor". He hinted that he favoured democracy, sparking speculations that he might move towards becoming a constitutional monarch. In many ways, however, what followed was an acceleration of the reform process that had been launched by King Hassan during the 1990s. This encompassed improved human rights, the fight against corruption and controlled political inclusion in the decision-making process but all driven from the top. The new King undoubtedly introduced a new style of government and showed a willingness to listen more closely to what people wanted. At the same time he made clear his opposition to Islamist extremism. In October 2001, the King announced his engagement to a 24-year old commoner, Salma Bennani, whom he married in Rabat on 21 March 2002 when he bestowed on her the title of Princess. She has since become patron of some charitable causes prominent among them support of needy cancer patients and research in the field. He ignored protocol when he publicly presented his new wife. He ordered the establishment of royal commissions to look into economic development, the problem of Western Sahara, employment and education. In fact, King Mohammed's approach to reform was similar to that of his father and all reforms were initiated from the top. He paid special attention to social deprivation and issues of human rights, releasing a large number of political prisoners soon after his accession. These included Abdessalam Yassine, the leader of the country's largest Islamic movement "Al Adl wal Ihsan", who was released from house arrest despite his scathing criticisms of both Mohammed VI and his father. The King strengthened the Consultative Council for Human Rights (Conseil Consultatif des Droits de l'Homme) and took further steps to bring Moroccan laws into line with international conventions and amended the penal code to abolish torture. He also acknowledged the government's responsibility for forced disappearances and other human rights abuses. Indeed, less than a month after his father's death he admitted government responsibility for the disappearances that had taken place during his father's reign and announced the formation of an Independent Arbitration Panel to review individual cases and award compensation to victims. This panel was disbanded in 2003, however, after paying compensation to some 4,000 victims. Subsequently, the King established the Instance Equite et Reconciliation (IER) to throw light on abuses committed between 1956 and 1999. There were questions as to whether these bodies went far enough in their investigations to close this chapter in Moroccan history. Often, little concern was paid to reconciliation and, for example, the IER could not compel testimony from the security forces while its mandate only covered the years up to 1999. Despite such criticisms, the IER represented an unprecedented initiative in the Arab world. It interviewed thousands of victims, conducted field investigations throughout Morocco, organised public hearings (many of which were broadcast on television, radio or the internet), and constructed a data base of the testimonies it had received. Most important, it aired issues of government responsibility for human rights abuses that had taken place.

MOUDAWANA

A major advance concerned changes to the Mudawana or family code that altered and enhanced the rights of women. The marriage age was raised from 15 to 18, women were allowed to divorce by mutual consent, it curbed the right of men to ask for divorces unilaterally and it restricted polygamy. The new code replaced the wife's duty of obedience with the concept of joint responsibility. These major changes to the traditional Muslim attitude towards women at first ran into fierce criticism from Islamist groups and there were massive demonstrations against the reforms in Casablanca. The fact that the King was also accepted by his people as the Commander of the Faithful gave him the authority to override Islamist opposition. There were problems of implementation – untrained judges and lack of information about their rights among women – yet the scope of the reforms represented a substantial breakthrough in the Muslim world. The reforms angered fundamentalists and terrorist bomb attacks in Casablanca in 2003 led to the enactment of new anti-terrorism laws and a reinvigorated campaign against extremists. As with all anti-terrorist legislation there were accusations that the new laws may have eroded human rights but the overwhelming majority of Moroccans prefer security and stability to extremism, public disorder and anarchy.

Although the new family law (Mudawana) was popular in many quarters, it met resistance in parliament, which initially refused to ratify it until the King intervened and asked both houses of parliament to pass the law.

In June 2000, Mohammed VI gave his first interview since becoming King to *Time* magazine. The interview focused upon the challenges that he faced. In answer to a question about advice that his father had given him, the King said: "To govern is not to please---. You will have to make decisions that will not please yourself nor please the people. But it will be for the welfare of the country." Speaking of the country's problems, the King listed unemployment and agriculture and emphasised the fight against poverty, misery, and illiteracy. On the issue of democracy the King said: "Morocco has a lot to do in terms of democracy. The daily practice of democracy evolves in time. Trying to apply a Western democratic system to a country of the Maghreb, the Middle East or the Gulf would be a mistake. We are not Germany, Sweden or Spain. I have a lot of respect for countries where the practice of democracy is highly developed. I think, however, that each country has to have its own specific features of democracy." Over the crucial question, "How do you assess Morocco's Islamist movement?" the King replied: "As Commander of the Faithful, it is out of the question that I fight Islam. We need to fight violence and ignorance. It is true, when one strolls out, one sees women with scarves and men with beards. This has always been the case in Morocco. Morocco is built on tolerance." On Europe, the King said: "We do not want Europe to assist us. We do not want Europe to give us handouts. All we ask is that Europe deals with us as a partner." On the question "Doesn't the Maghreb need to get its house in order?" the King was forthright: "There is a problem between Morocco and Algeria. There is no problem between Morocco and the Sahrawi Arab Democratic Republic [proclaimed by the Algerian-backed independence-seeking Polisario Front]. This is Algeria's creation. I refuse to take part in an Arab Maghreb Union meeting should the leaders, me included, enter into a contest on who will speak loudest."

During the first year of his reign (1999-2000), the King at once demonstrated his wish for reconciliation between the monarchy and the people and his desire for change. He adopted a populist style and was not afraid to speak out on social and economic issues, including the highly sensitive question of women's rights. He granted amnesty to thousands of prisoners and established an arbitration body to determine compensation for families of political opponents who had disappeared or suffered arbitrary detention. In December 1999 he dismissed the Interior Minister Driss Basri who had become identified with the authoritarian policies of his father's regime. In all these ways the King was signalling his desire for faster political change. At the same time that he modernised and changed the style of the monarchy, the King, who has been constantly on the move, also made plain that he intended both to reign and to rule. Thus, he dominated the political scene, made the appointments to all key posts and formulated national strategy. At the end of July 2001, on the second anniversary of his accession, the King reaffirmed his commitment to reform. He also said he wanted to promote the country's regional and cultural life. Speaking on the fifth anniversary of his accession in July 2004, the King said the strengthening of democracy was "irreversible" and insisted that there had to be a clear separation between religion and politics "to protect religion from discord and dissent". He emphasised that under the Moroccan constitution religion and politics were united only in the person of the monarch as Commander of the Faithful. The King was following an enlightened approach to the country's many problems while ensuring that no institution had the capacity to curb his authority. He has the power to appoint the prime minister and dissolve parliament. Important decisions are all taken by the "palace" and their execution lies with the royal entourage. Reforms have been driven by the desire for modernisation of the monarchy rather than for popular participation or government accountability. The King remains the dominant religious and political authority in the country and is the principal source of change and reform. All the new measures of his reign have been introduced from the top and none imposes any limits upon royal power. Although significant changes have been made in a democratic process, there is still the question whether these changes will lead to limitations upon the King's power. In 2006 *Der Spiegel* assessed the changes that had taken place since Mohammed VI had come to power and focused upon religion. It claimed that religion was making a comeback in Morocco and that more and more young, well-educated Moroccans were devouring the Koran. "The new piety, no longer limited to the mosque or prayers at home, is evident in full public view. More and more women are wearing headscarves, even in Casablanca's western fashion enclaves and Rabat's gleaming shopping centres." The article argued that the King had discovered religion as a means of modernising his society and progress through piety seemed to be the order of the day. "By granting new rights to women and strengthening civil liberties, the ruler of this country of 30 million on Africa's northern edge, which is 99 per cent Muslim, plans to democratise Morocco through a tolerant interpretation of the Koran."

The fact that the King belongs to the second oldest royal dynasty (after that of Japan) in the world as well as being Commander of the Faithful, confers great authority upon him. The Council of Religious Scholars, which the King established in 2004, has issued fatwas on some of the most important issues of the day and these, perhaps surprisingly, have been accepted by both young people and the old Islamists. If the King maintains his level of reforms, Morocco could become a model of democratic Islam. What Mohammed VI seeks is a delicate balance between Islamic tradition and the demands of a globalised world. This will not easily be achieved but what has been set in motion may just yield positive results if the continued political will remains.

Modern economic development has been central to the King's reforms and great efforts have been made to attract investment. This has meant removing obstacles to the promotion of investment. The labour code has been reformed and much attention has been paid to social dialogue and the creation of a social climate that is both healthy and competitive. Regional Investment Centres have been established while efforts have been made to reduce bureaucratic delays so as to safeguard the efficiency of business justice and improve governance and management systems. Morocco has entered into trade agreements with the EU and various neighbouring countries as well as the United States. As Morocco sees it, the reduction of gaps between the north and south of the Mediterranean presents an urgent challenge. More than ever, Morocco needs a Euro-Mediterranean partnership that includes a vast free trade zone and establishes a real common space that is mutually beneficial to the two sides. Morocco's economic policy, is set out in The Report: Emerging Morocco in 2007 by the Oxford Business Group, which sees the development of infrastructure and the widening of access to basic services such as education, training and health, as well as the struggle against poverty and exclusion, to be necessary conditions for the improvement of the competitiveness of the economy and the participation of everyone in meeting the challenges of human development and the creation of wealth. Great emphasis is placed upon education since examples throughout the world reveal that social development and the improvement of systems of governance are not merely accompaniments of development policies: they are, in fact, an essential pre-requisite for development. The pace of structural and institutional reforms is accelerating and such reforms are necessary for the success of the country's economic initiatives as well as its integrated vision of development. As the King has described Morocco's policy: "Our approach has been one of authentic democracy, whose cardinal virtue is to allow the actors directly concerned to invest themselves in the treatment of the important projects of the nation. The result is that decisions on major questions, which are pivotal for the nation, are conceived and constructed at the base and then refined and finalised at the summit."

Over ten years, Mohammed VI has made his presence felt throughout the country by touring the four corners of the Kingdom. Immediately on his accession, he changed both the nature of government and the speed with which he initiated and implemented changes. Expectations of coming changes were encouraged by the way the King moved constantly about the country, making contact with his subjects, rather than ruling from his palace. The King takes to the road with his entourage to visit regions where problems have to be overcome and development promoted. He concerns himself with everything: the building of roads to provide access for remote areas, the provision of electricity and clean drinking water, galvanising the creation of local facilities for health, education or sport. The King is highly visible and when visiting a place he remains for a fixed length of time while launching new projects or inspecting work that is in progress. Thus his reign has been described as one of proximity while Mohammed VI has been called a peripatetic king. One consequence of his constant movement is that visitors are often not received in the palace as they may have expected but instead meet the King on one of his tours around the country. Thus, the sovereign is as constantly concerned with the activities of his citizens as he is involved in affairs of state.

The achievements of the King's first years, which created a new climate in the country of political liberalisation and freedom to air grievances, after decades of tight control exercised by Hassan II, were in many respects symbolic: the righting of wrongs and the opening up of public debate. Openness of information is a weapon of fundamental change in the present world and King Mohammed showed his awareness of this in the message he sent to the Eighth Islamic Conference of

Information Ministers (ICIM) of the Organisation of Islamic Conference (OIC) in January 2009. He said information should be perceived as a productive sector in the new knowledge and communications-based economy. "Information" he said "is the weapon of modern times." He called for efficient planning to enable the voice of the Islamic world to be heard. Their objectives could only be met if they adopted an open attitude towards modern information and communication technology and promoted a give-and-take interaction with advanced nations and protect the Islamic world against negative influences. King Mohammed said it was absolutely necessary to lay the groundwork for bridging the digital gap between developed countries and OIC member states so that "our citizens may gain access to knowledge, which is the gateway to development, progress, cooperation and joint action."

Despite the achievements of his first ten years as a reformer, King Mohammed faces formidable tasks and challenges ahead. He cannot do everything himself and needs other reformers, civil society and ministers with real independent power to initiate and carry out changes for there are powerful conservative forces in Morocco that do not favour some of the King's initiatives. Ultimately, the King's reputation will depend upon the extent to which he will progressively share power with other people, groups and organisations for the benefit of his country.

CHAPTER FOUR: POLITICS AND GOVERNMENT

In September 2001, the King replaced Ahmed El-Midaoui as Interior Minister with the technocrat Driss Jettou who was a close royal ally. Jettou's appointment was seen as an attempt to improve the image of the monarchy in the run-up to legislative elections, which the King had scheduled for the autumn of 2002.

Parliament

The September 2002 elections followed changes in the electoral system that substituted proportional representation for first-past-the post, and also set aside 10 per cent of the 325 seats in the legislature for women. Following the elections, the Socialist Union of Popular Forces (USFP) won 50 seats and the Istiqlal 48 seats. The King had been expected to choose a new prime minister from the USFP leadership but instead named the technocrat and former Interior Minister Driss Jettou as prime minister and called on him to consult all parties to form a coalition government.

More than 20 parties had competed in the elections and the Islamic Party of Justice and Development (PJD) had become the third political party in the country after the Socialist USFP and the former independence party the Istiqlal.

At the opening of parliament that October, the King announced the outlines of a new family code. The code would include the legal status of Moroccan women with emphasis upon the equality of the sexes. This was a highly controversial issue that had given rise to bitter debate in 1997 between traditionalists and modernisers. However, on this occasion the opposition did not reject the code. In the course of 2004, the King announced the details of a new bill to regulate political parties: it banned any party founded on the basis of religion, ethnicity or region, or that aimed at impugning Islam, the monarchy or Morocco's territorial integrity. In a speech at the opening of Parliament in 2005, the King claimed that new legislation would strengthen political parties and facilitate the construction of a democratic society. He called upon the political parties to incorporate new elite and initiate new generations

Political parties in the House of Representatives following the 7 september 2007 general elections:

Istiqlal Party (PI)	52 seats
Justice and developement party (PJD)	46
Popular Movement (MP)	41
National Rally of Independents (RNI)	39
Socialist Union of Popular Forces (USFP)	36
Constitutional Union (UC)	27
Party for Progress and Socialism (PPS)	17
Front of Democratic Forces (FFD)	9
Social and Democratic Movement	9
Union of the National Democrat Party (PND) and Al-Ahd parties	14
Union of the PADS-CNI-PSU parties	6
Labour Party	5
Environnement and Developement Party	5
Equity and renewal Party	4
Socialist Party	2
Moroccan Union for Democracy	2
Citizens Forces	1
Liberty Alliance	1
Citizen and Developement Initiative	1
Renaissance and vertu Party	1
Independents	5

into democratic participation.

The elections of 2007, eight years after the King's accession to the throne, were significant for several reasons. The legislature is directly elected for a five-year term and on this occasion and to service the 15.5 million eligible voters a total of 38,687 polling stations were opened across the country. However, a low turnout was thought to reflect voters' unease at some of the reforms that had been carried out or the sense that the political parties were not sufficiently credible. The turnout was 37 per cent compared with 52 per cent in 2002. Abbas El Fassi, leader of the conservative Istiqlal Party, was appointed prime minister and proceeded to form a four-party coalition to obtain a majority in the 325-strong House of Representatives. The moderate Islamist Justice and Development Party (PJD) came second with 47 seats; a total of 33 parties had taken part in the elections. The PJD, which was by then ten years old, derived its support from the poorer districts of the big cities. It did not have strong grass roots support in the rural areas where the traditional parties – Istiqlal, the Popular Movement and the Socialist USFP – hold sway. Fear of terrorism is an important factor in Moroccan politics and failed attempts at suicide bombing in Meknes and Casablanaca made voters reluctant to support an Islamist party. Such fears were reinforced by events in neighbouring Algeria where, two days before the polls, a suicide bomb in Batna killed 20 people and injured many more; this was followed by another incident at Dellys, east of Algiers in which 30 people were killed and 50 injured. Al-Qaida claimed responsibility. Moroccans have been fearful of terrorism since the 16 May 2003 suicide bombings in Casablanca that killed 45 people.

Following his appointment as prime minister, El Fassi formed a coalition composed of four major parties as well as further support from 10 independent members. The distribution of portfolios in the 34 member government was as follows: Istiqlal nine portfolios plus the prime minister; the National Rally of Independents seven portfolios; the Socialist (USFP) five portfolios; and the Party of Progress and Socialism (PPS) two portfolios.

Despite the low turnout, the elections were free and fair. However, the electoral performance raised a number of important questions. First: the low turnout of only 37 per cent demonstrated a lack of confidence in the candidates and their parties. Second: the moderate Islamist PJD emerged in a position to act as a buffer against Al-Qaida inspired groups that seek to mobilise the poor and the marginalized. Third: the fragmentation of parties – 33 in all – ought to be corrected by the formation of larger, more comprehensive parties. Fourth: there was a growing demand for the abolition of the second chamber of councillors as it was seen to impede or delay legislation passed by the House of Representatives. Fifth: doubts were raised as to whether the coalition government could deliver on the promises of improved living standards, poverty reduction, job creation, education and reducing corruption. Performance would be enhanced according to how the PJD shaped up as the main opposition party to the government. The government faced many challenges: economic and social development, the settlement of the Western Sahara issue, relations with Algeria, the ever-present threat of terrorism, consolidating links with the EU, and improving relations with other African states. Prime Minister El Fassi had promised bold reforms, poverty reduction and anti-corruption measures. However, ultimate power and leadership resides with the King whose backing would be essential to any significant economic restructuring.

System of Government

Morocco's political system is laid down in the Constitution. Article I states: "Morocco shall have a democratic social and constitutional Monarchy as a system of government." Articles 2 to 18 spell out the rights of the people. Chapter Two (Monarchy) comprises articles 19 to 35, which set out the powers and duties of the King. Article 19 stipulates that the King "shall be the guarantor of the perpetuation and the continuity of the State. As Defender of the Faith, He shall ensure the respect for the Constitution. He shall be the Protector of the rights and liberties of the citizens, social groups and organisations." Article 23 states. "The person of the King shall be sacred and inviolable." Article 39 states, "No member of Parliament, shall be pursued, prosecuted, arrested, put into custody or brought to trial as a result of expressing opinions or casting a vote while exercising office functions, except when the opinions expressed may be injurious to the monarchical system and the religion of Islam or derogatory to the respect owed the King." It is a reasonable and apparently just constitution with the proviso that overriding power lies in the hands of the King. Participation is the essence of effective politics and the low turnout for the 2007 elections suggested a damaging indifference to the political process on the part of many would-be voters. As Imrane Binoual argues, "Participation in Morocco's political process is in decline, according to a recent study. Despite greater political openness in parties and labour organisations, membership is down and abstention rates in national elections are on the rise." In a study "Political marketing and electoral realities" researchers found that "96 per cent of those surveyed claimed to have no political affiliation and 98 pert cent said they were not members of a trade union." The 2007 legislative elections saw some of the lowest voter turnout in Moroccan history, despite efforts by various political figures to encourage the public – and young people in particular – to get involved. Just 37 per cent of registered voters turned out to cast their ballots. In a bid to gain a better understanding of young people's political participation in all its aspects the Fulbright Alumni Association and the Moroccan-American Commission for Educational and Cultural Exchange (MACECE) held a debate on 18 October 2007. According to Mustapha Khalfi, a young member of the Justice and Development Party, "almost all sociological studies acknowledge that there is a wide gulf in Morocco separating young people from politics in general and political parties in particular. This means that any political reform or democratic initiative would lack a social basis to support it." The number of young people in Morocco is estimated at more than 11 million, or 36 per cent of the population but their involvement in parties and elections is very low. Khalfi gave three reasons for this situation: "First, there is a political factor linked to the vision underpinning the policies pursued and the role of the citizen in political activity. The second has to do with the ability of young people to shape the activity of parties. The third relates to the cultural values and the degree to which the culture of participation exists in politics." Faouzi Chaabi, a businessman and Member of Parliament representing the Party of Progress and Socialism, spoke of the reasons why he felt young people remain sceptical of politics: "Our political parties show a strong tendency to pursue votes, remaining off-limits to young people. There is a lack of internal democracy within these parties, which are also characterised by ageing leadership." However, Chaabi rejected the notion that young people are cut off from politics: "They are very active in universities; what is happening is that they are showing apathy towards elections, and a rift separates them from parties." Another participant, Fadoua Amrani, suggested that the education system failed to explain the political process adequately to young people and should be reformed. "In Morocco there is dysfunction in the educational system; when young pupils make the transition to university, they continue to be treated like schoolchildren." The debate certainly threw light on young people's attitudes to politics and the need to engage them in the political process. Morocco can reasonably claim to be one of the more stable countries in Africa and since the accession of King Mohammed

VI in 1999; it has witnessed considerable progress in civil and human rights. Despite Mohammed V's support for the radical African states at the beginning of the independence era, Morocco tended to remain aloof from many of the upheavals and tensions that swept Africa at that time although Hassan II became progressively more authoritarian in his behaviour during his long reign, pre-empting opposition by resorting, sometimes, to oppressive measures. Mohammed VI has pursued a different path and worked to sustain the position of the monarchy by policies that have enhanced its legitimacy and so lessened the chances of revolutionary opponents exercising a wide appeal. Considerable development has taken place since 1999 and there has been consistent economic growth, and reforms have been designed to allow Morocco to profit from globalisation rather than be steam-rolled by it. Morocco has entered into free trade agreements with several powerful partners – France (the most important trading partner), the EU and the United States. As a consequence Moroccan enterprises have necessarily become more efficient and therefore more competitive abroad. A Free Trade Agreement (FTA) with the United States came into being in 2006 and a second FTA with the EU in 2009. Morocco is bound to suffer from some adverse effects of the worldwide recession triggered by the credit crunch and the global financial crisis but on the whole believes it is in a reasonably strong position to weather the storm. However, Morocco's ability to maintain its current rate of development will depend upon political stability and holding at bay Islamist extremism and this in turn requires a broad national consensus in support of the government. Legislation passed in 2006 will turn the military into an all-professional force as conscription is abolished. Corruption in many aspects of public life remains an intimidating problem although enough progress in combating corruption persuaded the World Bank in 2006 to approve a loan of $120 million to help improve the management of public sector resources. Special emphasis upon merit and integrity at senior levels of government has contributed to the fact that cases of official corruption are relatively low. The government aims to ensure that future generations of civil servants are given sufficient training and supervision to ensure that they do not enter their careers assuming that they accept bribes at the expense of the public. A government that is not seen to be corrupt and clearly fights against corruption where this occurs has a greater chance of winning the support of the people and being sustained by it. The position of the monarchy is greatly strengthened in Morocco, an Islamic society, because the King is also Commander of the Faithful. Moreover, the monarchy has deep roots and the Royal Family traces its lineage back to the Prophet Mohammed. The present King is regarded as a just and pious man. There have been opposition calls for a greater distribution of wealth and a lessening of the gap between the extremes of wealth and poverty but policies adopted by the King have earned him the title "guardian of the poor". He has launched policies that target rural poverty by improving educational opportunities and initiated economic developments that should benefit those at the lower end of the social scale. Critics of the monarchy claim that these policies are self-serving for both the monarchy and the establishment and in part of course this is true but they can serve the public at the same time (that is the nature of politics). A form of controlled democracy is always better than forcing the opposition to go underground. The government has taken care not to drive the principal Islamist party, the Party of Justice and Development (PJD), underground but instead has allowed it to take on an opposition role and following the elections of 2007 the PJD formed the second largest bloc in Parliament so that it can exert a significant impact upon the formation of policy. The ability of the establishment to occupy the political middle ground is the key to the King's success in controlling the disparate elements in the country. Justice and Charity (Justice et Bienfaisance) is a grassroots organisation and is peaceful in its political participation; however, it rouses government suspicions concerning its long-term intentions especially when it opposed reforms in favour of women. It is not registered as an official party but has expanded its recruitment drive for members. Sharia law influences but does not dictate policy. The King's liberal perspective on women's rights has been adopted, though not without initial opposition and ongoing conservative reluctance, and it means a greater involvement and participation by women in a whole range of activities. Those who oppose the present system of government claim that the King has too much power although this power is conferred upon him by the constitution. The King is fully aware of the world in which he lives and if real demands were made by the Moroccan people that he should cede more of his authority under a changed constitution, he would do so, though no one willingly surrenders power. However, such an eventuality would only arise if the political parties were much stronger than is the case at present. Morocco is not a revolutionary society but a conservative one although conservatives do not claim to be so in face of reforms that are pushed by the King. As one observer puts it, "in the past radicals went among the people to obtain support for their ideas although today young radicals simply argue with each other." During the ten years of the present King's rule there have been important reforms but no meaningful transformation to a fully Western-style democratic system. This raises the question as to whether the reforms that have been initiated so far make further change inevitable. How much is Morocco bound to respond to pressures exerted by foreign powers for greater democracy? In terms of *Realpolitik* these countries may pay lip service to democracy but their first concern is for a stable Morocco, both as a trading partner and for the US as a strategic partner as well. The King's reforms have been driven by the desire to modernise and make the monarchy acceptable in a media dominated age rather than to bring about popular participation and government accountability. In other words, the King remains the dominant religious and political authority in the country and the source of the reform process and all new initiatives for change are introduced from above and none of these reforms have diminished the King's power. When the King has changed the system of government, it has been in order to make it more efficient, modern, transparent and up-to-date. At present there are no serious challenges to royal power. There is a political triangle: the King with full executive power; the old political parties that have been asked to form the government; and the Islamists who at present are quiescent but remain the most likely source of real opposition and are feared by both the King and the old political parties. Meanwhile, Morocco with Lebanon is one of the two most open Arab states and of the two Morocco is by far the most stable.

CHAPTER FIVE: FOREIGN POLICY

Morocco's geographic location governs its foreign policy. It is only separated by 18 kilometres of the Gibraltar Straits from Spain; it has a colonial history with both France and Spain; it lies at the western extremity of the Arab world; because of this position it has come to be seen by the United States as a strategic ally of great importance. The Kingdom's foreign policy is conservative and pro-Western and Morocco sees itself as a link between Arab countries and the EU and the United States: it has a foot in both camps.

The European Union

Morocco has a positive image in Europe and its relations with the European Union are being consolidated. At present it is the only country to enjoy a special status with the EU, including a Free Trade Agreement. To encourage EU participation in its economic growth, Morocco needs to put in place a working and effective financial and technological infrastructure, which it is in the process of doing. It is regarded as a reliable partner by both the EU and individual EU member states, which see it as a safe country in which to invest and with which to trade. Morocco has close trading relations with France and Spain. In March 2000, King Mohammed VI visited Paris and asked for French support for Morocco's request for a partnership deal with the EU and this was finally granted in December 2008. The EU, for its part, seeks to develop particular close relations with Morocco, its geographical neighbour, and to support Morocco's economic and political reforms. This relationship emphasises close cooperation on democratic reform, economic modernisation, and migration issues. The development of EU-Morocco relations has been spelled out in an Action Plan under the European Neighbourhood Policy. Morocco and the EU are now bound together legally by an Association Agreement. In 2008 the EU offered Morocco "advanced status" relations under which Rabat would benefit from "all" the advantages of the bloc except for its institutions. Though "advanced status" carries no legal weight, it will nonetheless place Morocco a notch above the other members of the EU's "neighbourhood policy" – Egypt, Israel, Georgia and the Ukraine. This special relationship has been sought by Morocco for years since it will provide greater access for Moroccan products in the EU internal market.

Morocco's Foreign Minister Taieb Fassi Fihri told journalists: "This European engagement on the advanced status is firstly proof of confidence... in Morocco's efforts in terms of political reforms, consolidation of the rule of law, a better justice system, economic reforms, social cohesion and the fight against poverty." The new status was to mean everything except for the institutions. Under the terms of the advanced status, EU-Morocco summits will be held regularly to enhance political ties and Morocco will also participate in European civil and military crisis management operations. The advanced status will also include the establishment of a "common economic space" based on the rules of the European Economic Area, comprising the EU nations plus Iceland, Lichtenstein, Norway and Switzerland. In addition, Morocco will be able to participate in a number of EU agencies such as Europol, the European Air Security Agency and the European Monitoring Centre for Drugs and Drug Addiction. To help it attain this "advanced status", the EU will increase its aid to Morocco, which is already the biggest beneficiary of European Neighbourhood policy funds, with 607 million euros ($893) earmarked for the 2007-2010 period. Of the various issues of particular concern to the EU, illegal immigration and terrorism have risen to the top of the agenda to replace trade, especially agriculture and fisheries, and drug trafficking. Intelligence sharing and border control cooperation between the EU and Morocco began on a closer basis in 2000. Bilateral relations between Morocco and the EU have progressed remarkably over recent years with Morocco being allocated some 4 billion Dhs in subsidies. During 2009, the EU is expected to play a larger role in sector-specific support programmes aimed at reforming health care, boosting investment and exports, implementing an education strategy, cleaning up Morocco's water supply and curbing pollution. "This is a reflection of the EU's plan to support Moroccan development and boost cooperation between Morocco and the EU. These efforts will benefit both parties," said the EU ambassador to Rabat, Bruno Dethomas. Over 2.5 billion Dhs were spent under programmes adopted in 2008. The money went into projects as diverse as energy, roads in rural areas, public administration, basic health care and literacy. All together, 2008 was an especially important year for EU-Moroccan relations, as Dethomas pointed out in February 2009. It witnessed the adoption on

13 October of the joint document on Advanced Status, which lays down an ambitious road map for political, economic and social co-operation. For the first time there now exists a clear goal of achieving convergence with the acquis communautaire (body of EU laws and regulations) and greater involvement of civil society. The EU offered Morocco 317 million euros of "support": of that sum, 86m was assigned to the health sector, 93m to education, 50m to water and sanitation, 8m to the implementation of the recommendations of the Commission of Equity and Reconciliation, 60m to support investment and exports, and 20m to support the partnership programme with the EU. The EU will also grant Morocco 115m euros for the fiscal year 2010, to be allocated as follows: the agricultural sector 40m, improved access to remote areas 25m, judicial reform 20m and vocational training 30m. According to Jawad Kardoudi, president of the Moroccan Institute of International Relations, "The aim of the Advanced Status is to integrate Morocco into the European economic area, but this will require harmonisation of national legislation to bring it into line with European standards, particularly in areas of safety, hygiene and quality." What became clear through 2008 was the strategic location that Morocco occupies in the Euromed partnership.

France

In October 2003, French President Jacques Chirac visited Morocco for the first time since King Mohammed VI had come to the throne. More important for Morocco was the visit four years later in October 2007 of France's newly elected president Nicolas Sarkozy, which led to the signing of more than 2 billion euros ($2,8bn) of civilian and military contracts. The leading agreement was a draft accord for the construction of a high-speed TGV train between the cities of Tangiers and Casablanca. Half the estimated construction costs of euros2bn would go to the French group Alstom, the manufacturers of the high-speed train; the rail operator would be SNCF and RFF the network manager. Before this particular deal, Alstom had only exported the TGV outside Europe to South Korea. The first section of the TGV between Tangiers and Kenitra was scheduled to go into operation in 2013. The line will reduce travel time between Tangiers and Casablanca from five to just over two hours. The company also agreed to a 200m

President Sarkozy, wife Carla Bruni, Prince Moulay Rachid and King Mohammed VI

euros contract to supply 20 Prima locomotives and to build a power plant near the city of Oujda in the north east of the country. Under the terms of a further contract France sold Morocco its first advanced European multi-mission frigate (FREMM) for 500 million euros. The warship is identical to those in the French national fleet. Other contracts covered the modernisation of 25 Puma helicopters and 140 armoured vehicles and border surveillance equipment. The French nuclear energy firm Areva signed a draft agreement with Morocco's OCP for the extraction of uranium from phosphate acid. France also agreed to provide Morocco with civil nuclear power technology, and to assess suitable sites for plants, some of which could power desalination of seawater. The strong Franco-Moroccan relationship led to another agreement in the transport sector. France agreed to provide a $240m loan to finance the construction of a tram system in Rabat. On a three-day state visit to cement relations between their two countries, President Sarkozy and his business entourage certainly accomplished a great deal. King Mohammed and his younger brother met President Sarkozy in Marrakech. The President emphasised the importance of Morocco to France. Sarkozy elaborated on his idea of a new Mediterranean Union in which the King had expressed an interest. Another more controversial issue between the two countries was the fact that Morocco is a main target for African migrants seeking to gain access to Europe. The two countries also signed accords on judicial cooperation including one that would allow prisoners with dual French-Moroccan nationality to choose in which country they would serve their sentences. President Sarkozy was accompanied by his then Justice Minister, Rachida Dati (of Moroccan origin), as well as 70 business leaders.

In a speech, Sarkozy pledged France's help in setting up a civilian nuclear subsidiary. France would build a reactor to furnish electric power for the industrial town of Safi on the Atlantic coast. He said: "Future energy sources should not be the exclusive domain of more developed countries as long as international conventions are respected everywhere." Morocco has no gas reserves but it does have phosphates, its principal ore export. According to a French official, mixing economics with politics, nuclear power would help Morocco develop and "if Morocco develops, it can fight against (Islamist) extremism." In fact, the Moroccan security forces already exercise a tight rein over the kind of fundamentalist movements that emerged in Algeria due to poverty and unemployment during the 1990s.

France is a particularly strong supporter of Moroccan industry and is the country's largest trading partner, accounting for 17.8 per cent of its trade and France used its influence within the EU to have Morocco awarded "advanced" status for trade with the bloc. France gains substantially from its Moroccan "alliance" which is by no means one-sided. It gives credibility to France's new stance towards Africa, provides France with a convenient market for its exports and is a major holiday destination for French tourists. France as a major power has the closest relations with Morocco. These are based in part on history, language and affinityy but also it is to their mutual advantage to have close relations based upon trade, investment and security. France is the major source of arms for Morocco and these include Dassault Aviation's Rafale jet fighter. The intelligence and law enforcement agencies of the two countries exchange information and assist each other's investigations.

Morocco's pursuit of good relations with the EU and its individual member countries is enhanced by its close ties with France. After he had become President of France in 2007, Nicolas Sarkozy proposed a "Mediterranean Union" of 46 European, Middle Eastern and North African countries. Some saw this as a ploy to placate Turkey while keeping it out of the EU but Rabat saw it as an opportunity to expand its relations with its European partners. The Union as proposed by Sarkozy would be primarily an economic community whose members would consult on trade, immigration, security and energy. Morocco insists that it favours all forms of cooperation whether with Africa, Arab countries, the EU or the United States. It is Morocco's pivotal geographic position that encourages it to pursue both an EU policy and close relations with the US, more so, perhaps, than with Arab or Sub-Saharan African countries.

Spain

In May 2000, Spain's Prime Minister, Jose Aznavar, visited Morocco and in September King Mohammed VI visited Madrid; it seemed possible that a new era of normal relations between the two countries could begin. Unfortunately, in 2002, a dispute arose over the ownership of the tiny island off Morocco's coast that the Spanish call Perejil and

Moroccans Leila. The dispute is important because it highlights some of the points of grievance in EU-Islamic/African relations. Morocco regards itself as "relatively" pro-western while Spain sees itself as a bridge to the Arab world through Morocco. The island (Perejil/Leila) is only 200 metres from the Moroccan coast in the Straits of Gibraltar and lies in Morocco's territorial waters. It is about the size of a soccer pitch. The island has had no human inhabitants for more than 40 years though Moroccan herdsmen sometimes take their goats there to graze.

On 11 July 2002, six Moroccan soldiers raised their national flag on the island. Morocco claimed they were there to prevent the island being used by drug smugglers, illegal immigrants or terrorists. Following protests by the Spanish government, Moroccan navy cadets replaced the soldiers and then installed a fixed base on the island. This further incensed the Spanish government and both countries reiterated their claims to the island. On 18 July 2002, Spain launched Operation Recover Sovereignty at a cost of nearly 1 million euros. The operation, which involved the Spanish Navy and Air Force as well as the Commandos, was successful and the navy cadets were dislodged from the island without offering any resistance to the Spanish Commando attack force. Morocco's Foreign Minister, Mohamed Benaissa, described the Spanish operation as "an ignoble act, which amounts to an act of war." The scale of the Spanish operation produced a satirical headline in The British Newspaper the Daily Telegraph "Naval might defeats boys' slingshots." As soon as the operation had been completed the Spanish Commandos were replaced by members of the Spanish Legion. On 19 July, the United Kingdom's Financial Times denounced the Spanish action as "an act of folly" since "Europe does not need a new source of strain with the Arab World." The Spanish Legionnaires remained on the island until Morocco, following mediation by the United States, agreed to return to the status quo that existed previously so that, once more, the island was deserted. The status of the island is ambiguous and has been so since 1956 when Madrid's protectorate over nearby parts of Morocco came to an end. In 1415 Portugal seized the island. Portugal became united with Spain in 1580 (to 1640) but the island only came under Spanish control in 1668. At the present time Spain bases its claim to the island on the fact that it was not included in Morocco's independence treaty. Morocco insists that the question of ownership has never been settled. On 19 July 2002, Spain's El Pais published a long treatise on the history of Spain's North African territories, and concluded that Perejil/Leila belonged to Morocco. Then, Martin Waller, chief international correspondent for the United Press International news agency, wrote: "Morocco's claims over Perejil --- can expect a sympathetic hearing at the United Nations." The EU backed Spain but called on Madrid and Rabat to renew talks to find a long-term solution to the problem. NATO also backed Spain as a member state. Both the Arab League and the Organisation of the Islamic Conference (OIC) said they considered the island to be part of Morocco. US officials, speaking off the record, said that Washington did not recognise either Spanish or Moroccan sovereignty over the island. Both the US and the UN offered to mediate but Ana Palacio, then Spain's Foreign Minister, said mediation was necessary only in complicated cases such as the Middle East or the Balkans whereas the case of Perejil/Leila was "clear cut". Spain was ready to talk with Morocco about a range of bilateral issues but not about the island in isolation.

Spain has major strategic interests in Morocco and its aid for the INDH programme provides an opportunity to contribute to social stability in Morocco and to demonstrate that both Spain and the EU consider Morocco to be a priority country and to influence the country's current political and economic transition. Unfortunately, past imperialism keeps intruding to mar what otherwise could be a much more fruitful relationship. Thus, at the end of 2007, King Carlos of Spain visited the Spanish enclaves of Ceuta and Melilla. King Mohammed VI promptly denounced the visit and recalled Morocco's ambassador to Spain while his newly appointed Prime Minister, Abbas el Fassi, accused Spain of colonialism.

Much more positive, though the story goes back many years, is renewed Moroccan-Spanish interest in the construction of a tunnel across the Straits of Gibraltar to link Europe and Africa. The tunnel would boost both trade and general relations between the two countries but would also introduce a new set of problems concerning people and drug trafficking as well as a likely unequal flow of goods and people to the north. During 2006 the two governments drew up plans to bore a railroad under the Straits of Gibraltar. Should the tunnel come to fruition it would rank with such achievements as the Channel tunnel between Britain and France or the Panama canal. After years of studies and geological tests Spain and Morocco moved a step closer to realisation when they hired a Swiss engineering company to draft blueprints for an underwater rail route. Many obstacles remain to be overcome but optimists suggest the project could be completed by 2025. Assessments by government officials on both sides of the Mediterranean believe the tunnel would give an enormous boost to the economies of Southern Europe and North Africa. There are other considerations such as uniting two continents whose social and cultural differences are still immense. Karim Ghellab, Morocco's minister of transport and public work said, "We've already done a tremendous amount of work to make this dream come true, to go from an idea – a concept that is just philosophical – into something we can transform into reality. It's not easy to predict a date yet, but it is a project that will happen." It envisages a journey of 90 minutes from Tangiers to Seville. The tunnel would consist of twin tracks in parallel tunnels with a service tunnel in between and the trains would carry passengers as well as cars. The physical obstacles, however, are immense. At the shortest route across the Straits, the tunnel would have to travel beneath 3,000 feet of water. An alternative route would be twice as long and that would still mean tunnelling beneath 985 feet of water. A further difficulty is that the seabed around Gibraltar is much more permeable than the hard chalk rock under the channel and this would probably mean the tunnel would have to be driven an extra 300 feet down to avoid leakage. Although both governments are committed to the tunnel idea engineering problems and costs present formidable obstacles to be overcome. The tunnel would unite two continents and that alone is a reason for constructing it. Both Morocco and Spain say they are fully committed to the tunnel.

According to Spain's Prime Minister Jose Luis Rodriguez Zapatero, speaking in 2007, his country was fully committed to the project, which, he said, "will be a great symbol of our times" and "will change the face of Europe and Africa. With support from members of the European Union, we can build this historic connection between the two continents." According to Moroccan transport minister, Karim Ghellab, "It's clearly desirable that Morocco and Africa are joined to Europe by a fixed link." However, there are plenty of sceptics who see the tunnel becoming a route for illegal immigrants or an escape route for young Moroccans who see no future for themselves in their own country. Despite such views, scientists and politicians in both countries believe the tunnel will become a reality. The big question is where the money will come from; costs have been variously estimated as between $8bn and $13bn.

Apart from France and Spain, Morocco seeks improved trade and other relations with the EU as a whole. Bilateral trade between Britain and Morocco in 2006 totalled £671 million with UK exports to Morocco rising to £290 million, making Britain the fourth largest exporter to Morocco after France, Spain and Italy. The British Middle East Association promotes trade to the Middle East and North Africa and in recent years has increased its drive for investment and trade with Morocco. Britain and Germany are both important sources of tourists to Morocco and an increasing number of Britons are investing in Morocco by buying second homes there. The establishment of 16 Regional Investment Centres in major cities across Morocco provides a welcome one-stop shopping centre for foreign firms seeking to do business in the Moroccan market.

The United States of America

Morocco is one of America's oldest and closest allies and it was fitting that one of the first visits overseas by King Mohammed VI was to Washington in 2000. In 1777, Morocco became the first country to recognise the independence of the United States and the Treaty of Peace and Friendship of 1787 between the US and Morocco remains America's longest unbroken treaty. It was renegotiated in 1836 and is still in force, constituting the longest treaty relationship in American history. A testament to the special nature of the US-Moroccan relationship, the American Legation in Tangiers (now a museum) is home to the oldest US diplomatic property in the world, and the only building on foreign soil that is listed in the US National Register of Historic Places. For more than 230 years, Morocco and the United States have maintained a strong political partnership, which has become especially important in today's world in which Western-Islamic relations are so often in confrontation.

Morocco has been regularly praised by Washington for the reforms carried out under Mohammed VI and then rewarded with a free trade agreement (FTA) though this was more a token of approval than a change that would actually make much difference to trade between the two countries. US-Moroccan relations are closely tied to US interests in the region. A vital consideration for Washington has been to maintain good relations with the Moroccan Monarchy for neither Hassan II nor Mohammed VI has ever opposed American activities in the region, either during the Cold War or more recently as the US military has sought to extend its reach into Africa by the creation of its Africa Command (AFRICOM). Apart from the issue of Western Sahara, where the US has no interests, Morocco pursues a conservative foreign policy and this fits in well with the US-Moroccan alliance. In terms of its policies in the Mediterranean region, and especially the spread of its military influence, Washington needs a friendly Morocco, which is strategically placed in relation to both North and Sub-Saharan Africa. However, US diplomats in Morocco have established good relations with the Justice and Development Party (PJD) since it is legal, moderate for an Islamist party, competes in a democratic way with other parties and is a significant player on the Moroccan political stage. By being diplomatically friendly with the PJD, the US can demonstrate that it is not opposed to Islamist organisations but only to extremism. The US does work to strengthen democracy in Morocco by providing training through two US non-government organisations (NGOs), the National Democratic Institute for International Affairs and the International Republican Institute, both of them tied to the US Democratic Party and the Republican Party respectively. The training on offer is available to all legal parties but seems unlikely to make much difference to the political system or the standing of the parties.

In 2004, the US designated Morocco a "major non-NATO ally". This designation, for example, has been extended by the United States to Australia, Egypt, Israel, Japan and Kuwait. One result is that Morocco gains access to Research and Development expertise from the US Defence Department and eligibility for certain sensitive weapons systems and ammunition; access to more generous financing terms for military procurement and the possibility of bidding on profitable contracts for the repair and maintenance of US military equipment. Of particular value to Morocco is French and American support over the question of Western Sahara so that the country is not isolated over this issue at the United Nations. Thus, talks between the United Nations, Morocco and the Polisario in 2007-08 received a major boost when the US Assistant Secretary of State David Welch, said: "We consider the Moroccan proposal to provide real autonomy for Western Sahara to be serious and credible."

Wherever the US enters into FTAs, the advantages are reaped by the US rather than the smaller partner. As *the Middle East Times* (15/11/2007) has pointed out, the FTA envisages reforms to investment in Morocco and intellectual property rights, customs regulation and changes to the judicial system and obligations to enhanced labour and environmental provisions. It is a familiar list of demands made by rich to poor countries in recent years and so far Morocco has gained little from the FTA. Thus, while Morocco requires the FTA to boost its economy and assist in raising living standards, the US sees the FTA as a means of enhancing regional security and stability. The aims are different and the likelihood is that one or other partner will be disappointed by the outcomes.

Nonetheless, Morocco is a long-standing ally of the United States, situated in a strategic position that offers major advantages to the more powerful ally and Rabat has a right to expect substantial economic returns from this unequal friendship.

Arab World

Morocco's foreign policy has often differed from that of its Arab neighbours and has officially been non-aligned although generally sympathetic to the West. Throughout the Cold War, Morocco generally sided with the Western European powers and the United States rather than with the Eastern bloc, whereas other Arab states, such as Algeria and Syria, chose to adopt a pro-Soviet position. Unhappily, relations with its Arab neighbour Algeria have been difficult if not antagonistic ever since independence in 1962.

Maghreb

At the EU-OAU summit in Cairo during April 2000, King Mohammed VI had talks with Algeria's President Abdelaziz Bouteflika but the Western Sahara issue prevented any accord being reached. In March 2005, the King attended the Arab League summit in Algiers, his first visit to Algeria. He again had private talks with President Bouteflika but no thaw in relations followed. Consequently, the following May, the King refused to attend the Arab Maghreb Union summit after

Bouteflika had reaffirmed Algerian support for the Polisario. Over most of the years since independence, Morocco's relations with Algeria have been poor, suspicious and sometimes downright hostile and confrontational, and there was sharp border fighting between the two countries in 1963. Both countries have sought to establish their primacy in the Maghreb but while Morocco's claim to regional leadership was based on its centuries old national identity that of Algeria rested upon its prestige in winning the independence war against France. However, much of their post-independence enmity derives from their dispute over Western Sahara, which Morocco claims as part of its historic territory prior to the partitions in the region carried out by France and Spain during the colonial era. Algeria, on the other hand, supported the Polisario movement that sought to establish a separate state. Repeated UN attempts to solve the Algerian-Moroccan deadlock have ended in failure. Algeria has constantly said that its border with Morocco will remain closed until the two countries have agreed a "package of deals", which really means a solution to the Western Sahara conflict. The border was closed in 1994 after Moroccan security forces arrested an Algerian who shot and killed two tourists in a hotel in Marrakech. Thereafter visa restrictions were imposed on Algerians travelling to Morocco.

In the new century terrorist attacks in both Algeria and Morocco brought a new dimension into the region of North West Africa. In 2004, Morocco waived visa restrictions for Algerians and Algeria reciprocated in 2005. Opening the border would strengthen security cooperation and benefit those families from either country that have been separated. One million Algerians live in Morocco. In economic terms the two countries complement each other and both would reap important advantages from economic exchanges. Algeria could supply Morocco with hydrocarbons – oil and gas – in exchange for agricultural and industrial products from Morocco. The closed border costs Morocco at least $1 billion a year in trade and tourism revenue. On 21 March 2008, the Moroccan Foreign Ministry in Rabat issued a statement about the border: "The Kingdom of Morocco calls, in fraternal friendship and total sincerity, for a normalisation of relations with Algeria, and for the opening of the borders between the two countries.

The next day, the Algerian Interior Minister Noureddine Yazid Zerhouni welcomed the Moroccan call for the reopening of the border but said the matter was not urgent: "The question of movement across the border cannot be separated from a global approach on how we want our Maghreb to be." He went on: "It is not a question of building a Maghreb where some win and others lose. The Maghreb is not limited to Morocco and Algeria. All the peoples who find themselves in this group should have their place." In fact both countries carry a lot of baggage from the past and though there may be deep-seated "core" issues between the two countries it is the business of governments to overcome these. Algeria seems set in its purpose not to do so. An entire generation has failed to come up with constructive ideas about how to come to an agreement. Both countries need economic complementarity and political coordination on the issue of the Maghreb Union and on how to react to the European Neighbourhood Policy. Instead, a new generation of policy makers is coming to accept a state of caution about the other, mistrust and economic, political and cultural misunderstanding.

The year 2008 was the fiftieth anniversary of the Tangiers Conference of April 1958 when Morocco's Independence Party, Algeria's National Liberation Front and Tunisia's Destour Party between them paved the way for the Maghreb Union at a time when they enjoyed a real sense of solidarity because they were each facing and resisting the last throws of French colonialism. Subsequently, the solidarity evaporated and the Union became little more than an aspiration. Although Morocco called for open borders and the normalisation of relations, this was rebuffed by Algeria. The Arabic daily *Assahra Al Maghribiya* said, "Since Morocco's announcement to open borders and normalise bilateral relations, Algeria has proved once again its persistence to keep borders shut on its side." The French language *L'Opinion* wrote, "Our neighbour continues to practice the headlong rush policy whenever there is a suitable opportunity to reach an honourable solution to the issue and turn its back whenever Morocco made a concession to defuse the crisis." The Arabic language *Bayan Al Yaoum* says that "Morocco's call is another initiative that shows to the countries region and the international community the Kingdom's readiness to close this page, build the Maghreb Union and face common security, strategic and development challenges." In a similar vein, the Algerian daily *Le Soir d'Algerie* claimed that the Algerian rulers "many of whom are descendants of the region at borders between Morocco and Algeria" know better than ever the aspirations of the border populations, namely "to meet in brotherhood and solidarity as before." It was clear at the time of this 50th anniversary of the Tangiers meeting that many Algerians wanted the border opened. Following Algeria's rejection of the Moroccan call to re-open their joint borders, Algerian opposition parties, *Front des Forces Socialistes* (FFS) and the *Parti des Travailleurs* (PT) voiced support for Morocco's call for the sake of the two peoples. The Algerian Labour Party said it supported the reopening of frontiers "because the Algerian and the Moroccan peoples need it." Djelloul Djondi, a leading member of the PT, said in a statement to the Algerian daily *Midi Libre*, this opening (of the border) would also benefit the Maghreb as a whole and he pleaded for reinforcing Moroccan-Algerian relations "to the benefit of the two peoples." In Morocco, there was an angry press reaction to the Algerian rebuff.

Middle East Peace

Historically, Morocco has played a significant role in the Middle East peace process, including participation in international peace conferences, hosting Israeli leaders in Morocco, and serving as an intermediary between Israel and other Arab states.

Morocco's long-term goals are to strengthen its active role in the Arab world, Africa and the Muslim world while maintaining close ties with Europe and the United States. Morocco has long tried to encourage Israeli-Palestinian negotiations while urging moderation on both sides. King Hassan II acted as mediator between the Palestinians and the Israelis and in 1986 invited the then Israeli Prime Minister Shimon Peres for talks, becoming the second Arab leader to host an Israeli leader after Egypt.

Morocco continues to play a significant role in the search for peace in the Middle East. For many years King Hassan II was acting chairman of the Arab League and the Organisation of the Islamic Conference's (OIC) Jerusalem committee. In May 1989, King Hassan hosted the Casablanca summit, which reintegrated Egypt into the Arab fold and endorsed a moderate approach to the peace process in the Middle East. Like his father, King Mohammed VI serves as chairman of the Islamic Conference's Jerusalem Committee and continues to state his position that Jerusalem be shared by Muslims, Christians and Jews, with East Jerusalem as capital of a sovereign Palestinian state.

Morocco maintains close, friendly relations with the Gulf States, especially Saudi Arabia and the United Arab Emirates. Following the invasion of Kuwait by Iraq in August 1990, Morocco was the first Arab state to condemn the action and sent troops to help defend Saudi Arabia against any further aggression. By December 1990, over 1,500 Moroccan troops were based in Saudi Arabia as part of the multinational force. Meeting in Agadir in May 2001, Morocco, Jordan, Tunisia and Egypt resolved to work for the establishment of an enlarged free trade zone encompassing the Arab Mediterranean countries. The free trade zone agreement, ratified in Rabat on 25 February 2004, serves as an example for other Arab and African groupings.

On March 6, 2009, Morocco severed diplomatic relations with Iran after comments made by an Iranian politician that Bahrain was

King Mohammed VI with Equatorial Guinea President Teodoro Obiang Nguema Mbasogo in Bata

historically part of Iran and as such still had a seat in the Iranian parliament. The government-owned Iranian media launched a vociferous campaign of denigration against Morocco's institutions and Rabat described the comments as an attempt to "alter the religious fundamentals of the Kingdom", and accused Tehran of attempting to spread Shia Islam. Morocco is a majority Sunni country and Bahrain, despite having a large shi'ite population, is ruled by a Sunni elite. Iran, a majority Shi'ite, reportedly has an interest in empowering the Shi'ites in Bahrain in order to raise its own status in the Gulf region. Morocco, a staunch ally of the Gulf States, will not tolerate any interference in their territorial integrity or internal affairs.

The King's friendship with King Abdallah of Jordan and King Abdullah ibn Abdul Aziz of Saudi Arabia and the fact that Morocco has a significant and influential Jewish minority as well as a strong Moroccan-Jewish minority in Israel may prompt Mohammed VI to play a more active role in mediation between Israelis and Palestinians by supporting more actively the American president Barrack Obama's efforts to reach a two state solution.

Africa

Although a founding member of the African Union (formerly the Organisation of African Unity), Morocco withdrew in November 1984 in protest at the controversial admission to the OAU of the Sahrawi Arab Democratic Republic. Nonetheless, Morocco remains involved in African diplomacy and economic activity and contributes consistently to UN peacekeeping efforts on the continent.

King Mohammed VI has adopted a vigorous new policy towards African countries and at the Cairo Europe-Africa Summit of 2000 he cancelled all debts of the poorest African countries and exempted their products from customs duties on entry to the Moroccan market. In 2003, Morocco signed 270 accords with African states, compared with only 88 accords between 1972 and 1985. It initiated programmes of cooperation covering agriculture, hydraulic engineering, urban planning, infrastructure, health and education. During Mohammed VI's reign, Morocco has worked to consolidate economic ties with Sub-Saharan Africa and has concluded trade agreements with 17 countries. In February 2001, Morocco joined the Community of Sahel-Saharan

States (COMESSA) at its third summit in Khartoum. In 2002, at Rabat, Morocco signed a trade and investment agreement with the West African Economic and Monetary Union (UEMOA). The king has paid a number of visits to African countries including Senegal, Mauritania, Benin, Cameroon, Congo, Gabon, Niger, The Gambia, Democratic Republic of Congo, Guinea and Equatorial Guinea. Between 1996 and 2008 Morocco's annual trade with Sub-Saharan Africa increased from $272 million to $450 million, still a very small proportion of the country's total trade. Despite considerable progress, trade policies in Sub-Saharan Africa remain broadly protectionist, maintaining a range of controls which inhibit the growth of trade. If the obstacles to increased trade could be overcome, Morocco's trade with Sub-Saharan Africa could easily top $1 billion a year. Even so, over the last decade Morocco has consolidated its position as a bridge between Africa and Europe. The Kingdom has been responsible for a number of initiatives to help its African partners. It has acted as spokesman for indebted countries, as chairman of the African group in the World Trade Organisation (WTO) and in the UN, and acted as leader of African countries in the Group of 77, while in June 2003 at Rabat, Morocco hosted the Extraordinary Conference of the Least Developed Countries.

Moroccan private investment in Sub-Saharan Africa is growing, especially in markets where its companies enjoy free business access. Most investments have been in banking, telecommunications, the cement industry, mining, transport and construction. Investors principally participate in local enterprises or set up subsidiaries. Moroccan banks, *Attijariwafabank* and *BMCE Bank* have spread their activities in a number of countries: *Attijariwafabank* has operations in Tunisia, Senegal and Mali while the *BMCE Bank* is present in Europe and Asia as well as 12 African countries. In 2007, *BMCE Bank* acquired 35 per cent of equity of Bank of Africa capital of the West African Economic and Monetary Union (UEMOA). Telecommunications represents 25 per cent of Morocco's foreign direct investment (FDI) and *Maroc Telecom* is a major shareholder of local operations in Mauritania, Burkina Faso and Gabon. Moroccan holding companies have investments in Tunisia, the Ivory Coast and Egypt and are looking at possible investments in Gabon, Equatorial Guinea and Mali. *Managem*, the mining subsidiary of *Ominium Nord Africain* (ONA), has acquired ore deposits in Guinea, Mali, Burkina Faso, and Niger. *Royal Air Maroc* has consolidated its commercial presence in Africa by opening international links through Casablanca airport with Benin, Burkina Faso, Cameroon, Congo, DR Congo, Equatorial Guinea, Gabon, The Gambia, Ghana, Guinea, Ivory Coast, Mali, Mauritania, Niger, Nigeria, Senegal, Sera Leone and Togo, a steady outward investment by Moroccan companies in an ever-widening circle of African countries.

Since 2000, Morocco has substantially deepened its economic ties with the rest of the African continent by investing in many African states while an increasing number of Moroccan companies set up operations in the region, according to the UNCTAD 2009 report on Economic Development in Africa. Moroccan mining companies are now present in Congo, Gabon, Guinea, Mali and Burkina Faso. Maroc Telecom, the national telecommunications company, has operations in Mauritania and Burkina Faso and Mali while Moroccan banks have established themselves in Tunisia and Algeria.

Ynna Holdings, a Moroccan company active in construction and manufacturing, has operations in Libya, Tunisia, Egypt, Côte d'Ivoire, Mauritania, Gabon, Mali and Equatorial Guinea.

The most important destination of Moroccan investment in Africa is Senegal where Moroccan transport companies are active such as the national shipping company COMANAV and the airline Royal Air Maroc, which have respectively taken over a passenger transport route and set up a new airline in partnership with the Government of Senegal.

Private Moroccan companies are also strongly present in Senegal in construction and public works, power, telecoms and the pharmaceutical industry. Since 2005, the UNCTAD report says, banks have also started to establish themselves strongly in the country, notably with the establishment of a subsidiary of Moroccan bank Attijariwafa, North Africa's largest bank.

Morocco is now playing a vital role in African education. It provides over 7,000 grants annually to students from 35 African countries as well as higher education training in prestigious academies and schools. Thousands of Africans graduate every year from Moroccan universities, military academies, journalism and engineering schools and as airline pilots and judges.

Morocco's top foreign policy priority remains its claim to the territory of Western Sahara.

The Moroccan Diaspora

There is a significant diaspora of Moroccans to be found principally in Europe and their remittances home amount to between $5 billion and $6 billion a year, so that they make a sizeable addition to the GDP. Some, though not enough of these overseas Moroccans, return with their training and new skills to help with the growth of the economy. However, as the government acknowledges, there must be available in Morocco sufficient opportunities and incentives to entice them to return. They represent an overseas capital to be drawn upon. One estimate suggests the diaspora could be as large as 4,500,000. Europe has long been the principal destination for Moroccan migrants and the biggest concentration of them is in France – an estimated 1,600.000. Another large group consists of 997,000 Moroccan Jews who have left the country in the years since the creation of the state of Israel to which they have emigrated though there is little likelihood that any of this group will be enticed back to Morocco in the future.

wMany Moroccans of the diaspora have been guest workers, especially in the Gulf States, and the policy of King Hassan II in encouraging a new generation of craft workers by his programme of restoring mosques and royal palaces produced a surplus of such workers, many of whom have been in high demand for similar decorative craft work in the Gulf.

Remittances from the Moroccan diaspora now make a substantial contribution to the economy. In the first eight months of 2007, for example, a total of $4.7 billion was transferred back home, and this represented a 15.5 per cent increase over the same period in 2006. In 2007 remittances soared by 42.6 per cent compared with the annual average for the period 2002-2006 when the figure was $3.3bn. Both real estate and tourism have benefited from the large number of Moroccans who live abroad. Real estate has witnessed a growing number of direct investments in property while tourism has received increased income from nationals who return home on holiday or family visits. Apart from Egypt, Morocco now receives more remittances than any other country in the Middle East or North Africa. Remittances from "Moroccans Resident Abroad" take different forms and have bolstered the economy in a variety of areas and ways. According to the *Conseil Deontologique des Valeurs Mobilieres* (CDUM), Morocco's capital market authority, 58 per cent of overseas investors in the Casablanca Stock Exchange (CSE) are Moroccan expatriates. Morocco's *Organismes de placement collectif en valeurs mobilieres* (OPCUM) mutual funds, drew in $1.68bn from overseas residents in 2007, representing 27.8 per cent of total investments in these organisations. In addition, of course, remittances have a traditional role of supplementing the incomes of expatriates' families and boosting foreign currency earnings. The steady increase in remittances from Moroccans resident abroad (MREs) bolsters ordinary citizens' incomes in the Kingdom and provides much needed investment in a range of developments. In the first half of 2008 remittances came to $3.5bn, an increase of 5 per cent over the same period for 2007.

About 3.3 million Moroccans live outside the Kingdom, nearly three times as many as 15 years earlier. However, although the diaspora is widening in the number of host countries, 80 per cent live in the EU (with France and Spain in the lead), which is the biggest source of remittances. About half the emigrants are female, and this reflects an increase in single women migrants. The Moroccan Centre for Economics claims "fund transfers made by Moroccan expatriates are a major consideration for the Moroccan economy, not just as a way of supporting household revenues, but also and more importantly, as a source of extra savings and an essential source of foreign currency." The government encourages its expatriates to invest more in the country. In August 2008, Morocco signed an accord to set up electronic money transfers through technology of the Universal Postal Union (UPU), the UN's postal agency. This agency is also used by Qatar and the UAE to which a growing number of Moroccans have emigrated. According to the UPU the system should help "improve access for rural populations to secure reliable money transfer services through formal channels." Recession in Europe may slow the rate and volume of remittances sent back to Morocco. Some Moroccan migrants are concerned about corruption and bureaucracy, so are reluctant to transfer home large sums. In 2009, with Spain's economy suffering, especially in the construction industry, there was growing fear that remittances from Spain would fall while other European countries such as France also face the adverse impact of the recession.

Europe's Moroccan diaspora figures:

France	1600,000
Spain	700,000
Italy	500,000
Netherlands	341,640
Belgium	333,244
Germany	202,000
UK	21,000
Sweden	20,000
Denmark	15,000
Switzerland	13,500
Norway	7,400

North America'a Moroccan diaspora:

USA	200,000
Canada	140,000

Arab countries Moroccan diaspora:

Algeria	164,000
Saudi Arabia	43,216
Kuwait	21,843

CHAPTER SIX: THE QUESTION OF WESTERN SAHARA

A sovereign State for many centuries, the Kingdom of Morocco was the exception among colonial territories in Africa and the Middle East when, briefly, it submitted to being French and Spanish protectorates (1912-1956) and it enjoyed its historical state as a Kingdom throughout the period of colonial rule. Although the Algeciras Conference in 1906 empowered Spain and France to develop their political and economic influence in Morocco, it, nevertheless, reiterated the "sovereignty and the independence of the Sultan as well as the integrity of his territories and economic freedom".

The Franco-Spanish Convention of 27 November 1912 was the document under which Western Sahara assumed its final status as a Spanish protectorate, leased to Spain by France following the Franco-Moroccan protectorate treaty of 30 March 1912.

Once independent, the joint Franco-Moroccan agreement of March 2, 1956 and that of Morocco and Spain of April 7, 1956 confirmed the "territorial unity" of the Kingdom.

Within a month of Morocco's independence, anti-Spanish demonstrations occurred regularly in the Saharan territories still under Spanish occupation. The attacks on Spanish garrisons by the Moroccan Liberation army were so fierce that Spanish troops were forced to retreat to Ifni, which became the capital of Spanish Sahara. Had it not been for sophisticated French weaponry, Spanish troops would have been overrun and driven out of the territory in the 1950s. The turning point was the combined Franco-Spanish military force that crushed the Liberation Army in operation Ecouvillion (sometimes referred to as Operation Ouragan) in February 1958 that drove most of the rebellious inhabitants north into Morocco proper.

This military offensive was designed to thwart any Moroccan attempts to defeat the colonial powers' interest in Western Sahara, Mauritania and Algeria. To reduce Morocco's anger, Spain ceded Tarfaya to Morocco on 1 April 1958 and then Ifni in 1969 but neither of these cessions in any way reduced Morocco's claims to Western Sahara. Instead, the Madrid government of Generalissimo Franco was strongly urged to speed up the decolonisation process of the Saharan territories and Western Sahara became the object of lengthy negotiations. Morocco even rejected a Spanish offer of all the Saharan territories in exchange for Morocco's recognition of Spanish sovereignty over the occupied Presidios (The Enclaves of Ceuta and Melillia). Morocco then launched an international initiative which resulted in the United Nations General Assembly taking up the case: Resolution 229 XX.1 was adopted on December 20, 1965 and was to serve as a model for those that followed until 1973, urging Spain to decolonise its North African territories. The resolution was applied to the enclave of Sidi Ifni as well as the "Spanish Sahara".

Two years later, another resolution was passed calling on the colonial power to hold a referendum to allow the population of the Sahara to determine their future. Spain refused to comply with these resolutions and preferred, instead, to maintain the status quo.

Growing international pressure and Morocco's determination to restore its usurped territories led Spain to return the enclave of Sidi Ifni to Morocco by virtue of the Fez Treaty of January 1969. This did not deter Morocco from lobbying for the complete decolonisation of the Saharan territories under Spanish occupation.

In August 1974, after the adoption of seven UN resolutions, Spain informed the United Nations that it would hold a referendum in Western Sahara in1975, to grant independence or integration with Spain to the population of the occupied territories. Morocco objected to a proposal that ignored its position and called for arbitration by the International Court of Justice (ICJ) for an advisory opinion on the pre-colonial legal status of the territory.

Spain's refusal to negotiate with Morocco over the decolonisation of Western Sahara was based on its claim that the territory had never been under Moroccan sovereignty and was without owner (terra nullius).

The UN General Assembly adopted resolution 3292 of December 13, 1974 requesting the ICJ to provide an opinion as to whether the territory belonged to no one at the time of colonisation by Spain in 1884 (terra Nullius) and what were the legal ties between the territory and the kingdom of Morocco and Mauritania.

The ICJ delivered its verdict of October 16, 1975 in which it ruled that the territory was not "terra nullius" and that a Moroccan political authority had been exercised over it. Furthermore, legal ties of allegiance existed between Morocco and the Western Sahara at the time of Spanish colonisation in 1884. The ICJ also said that the inhabitants of the area should be entitled to self-determination. According to Muslim Law "Sharia" allegiance means temporal and spiritual bonds between the population and the Monarch. Such allegiance means the establishment of a bond between the population and the Moroccan Monarch, a contract between the King and his people.

With regards to Western Sahara and Morocco, Islamic law remains paramount in the light of the juridical system in force in the region. The basis of this argument is embedded in the UN Charter, which forbids the use of threats or force against "the territorial integrity or political independence of any state". The UN Declaration on the granting of independence to colonial countries and peoples emphasised the point further: "Any attempt to destroy in part or in whole the national unity and territorial integrity of a country is incompatible with the aims and principles of the United Nations Charter". Therefore, despite the fact that partition of Moroccan territory was brought about by the Franco-Spanish treaties of June 27, 1900, October 3, 1904 and November 27, 1912, under no circumstances were the Moroccan authorities prepared to relinquish any territory to the colonial powers except as the result of armed force or outright occupation.

Colonial laws should not be accepted as legally binding or final for the simple reason that they were designed to serve the interests of the colonial powers and not those of the colonised territories or their inhabitants. The validity of treaties between foreign powers should only assume the force of law if the colonised state was a signatory to them and under no restriction or duress. This is clearly not the case with regards to Morocco and Western Sahara. In recognising the existence of legal ties of allegiance between the Moroccan monarchy and tribes in Western Sahara, the Court did in fact imply the territorial sovereignty between Western Sahara and Morocco since in Islamic law, sovereignty belongs to God alone and earthly sovereignty is conferred by a population's "Bay'a" (Allegiance). The absence of precise territorial limits to the Moroccan state was attributed to the Muslim concept of greater importance being given to the Sultan's political and religious authority over the inhabitants rather than political control over the territory. Morocco stands out as the exception among colonial territories in Africa with a historical state legitimacy which was for a long time derived from the ruling dynasty and it was only in the 19th century that nationhood began to be accepted as the legitimising principle.

Following the findings of the ICJ and the established Moroccan claim of legitimacy, 350,000 unarmed Moroccan civilians holding the holy Koran, marched peacefully into the Western Sahara on November 6, 1975. The "Green March" forced Spain to negotiate and the march was halted on November 9 when the Moroccan Monarch ordered the marchers to return to the point of departure. The outcome was the Tripartite Madrid Agreement (Spain-Morocco-Mauritania) of November 14, 1975, reached in accordance with Article 33 of the United Nations Charter and Resolution 380 of the Security Council, which on 6 November had invited the parties concerned to negotiate. The accord was satisfactorily registered with the UN General Assembly in its Resolution (3458 B XXX) of December 10, 1975. The Agreement was also approved by the "Jemaa", an assembly consisting of notables and representatives of all the tribes in the Western Sahara. The Madrid Accord provided for the withdrawal of Spanish Troops from the occupied territories by February 26, 1976 but the treaty was condemned by Algeria's rulers who proclaimed the "Saharan Arab Democratic Republic" (SADR) on their territory in February 1976 and attempted through armed guerrilla attacks by the Polisario, to enlist opposition to the Moroccan regime and threaten the stability and security of the region. Morocco argued that the "Jemaa" was the authentic representative body of the Sahrawi population while Algeria supported the claim of the Polisario to fulfill this role.

A Moroccan-Algerian armed confrontation took place in Amghala, in Western Sahara, on January 19, 1976 when 136 Algerian soldiers were captured to be released in May 1987.

When King Hassan II (1961-1999) urged President Boumedienne (1965-1979) of Algeria either to declare war on Morocco or refrain from interfering in Morocco's internal affairs, Boumedienne's military machine embarked on a recruitment drive of mercenaries from the drought and famine stricken Sahel. Algeria's involvement in Western Sahara was translated into aggressive arming, training and providing the Polisario with a base in Tindouf, in South-West Algeria, from which to oppose the Moroccans. Algeria then launched a worldwide political and diplomatic campaign to get Western Sahara recognised by as many states as possible so as to face Morocco with the fait accompli of a "republic" that in fact only existed on Algerian soil. Hit and run tactics were adopted by the guerrillas and the Moroccan-Algerian dispute reached a climax when Colonel Gaddafi of Libya, who initially supported Morocco's claims, switched sides and both offered his full support to Algeria and also provided financial and military assistance to the Polisario, thus further heightening the tension in the North-West African region.

Gaddafi claimed to have founded the Polisario and his assertion was confirmed by the first secretary general of the Polisario, El Wali Mustapha Sayed, who said at a press conference in Tripoli on 29 October 1975, "we came to Libya barefoot, we left armed". The Libyan leader confirmed his ties with the Polisario in a letter to King Hassan II on 27 February 1976 stating that his country "fulfilled its Arab duty by providing the Polisario with arms and an office in Tripoli".

The Saharan question figured in the Organisation of African Unity's (OAU) agenda from 1976 onwards and almost proved fatal to the existence of the Pan-African Organization. A possible breakthrough came about when, at the Nairobi OAU Summit in June 1981, King Hassan II proposed a referendum in the Saharan territory in accordance with the OAU's ad hoc Committee recommendations. Hopes of a settlement were soon dashed by the Polisario guerrillas' attacks on the Moroccan Garrison of Guelta Zemmour on October 13, 1981 when Sam missiles were used to shoot down Moroccan aircraft. Control of the sophisticated Sam-8 missiles was believed to have been the work of Cuban military instructors. Cuban involvement had already been confirmed when Moroccan patrol boats seized a Cuban ship off the Western Saharan Coast. The most damaging blow to the OAU's efforts to settle the dispute came at a ministerial meeting in Addis Ababa in mid-February 1982, when the Secretary General of the Pan-African organisation, Mr Edem Kodjo, made the unilateral decision to admit "SADR" as a member state without prior consultation with the OAU Implementation Committee, chaired by Kenyan President Daniel Arap Moi. This controversial decision led to the walk out of 19 member states demanding that it must be revoked before any OAU activities could be resumed. The chaos caused by Kodjo's move led to the paralysis of all activities of the Pan-African organisation. His decision was disapproved both by the then OAU chairman and also by his own country, Togo. It destroyed any possibility of a peaceful solution at that time. Kodjo based his argument for the recognition of SADR on the support of 26 of the 50 OAU members but his critics pointed out that it was for an Assembly of Heads of State and Government, the supreme organ of the OAU, to make such a decision.

The Moroccans, for their part, pointed to article 27 of the OAU Charter which calls for a two-thirds majority instead of a simple majority as the SADR did not fulfill the requirements of a sovereign and independent state. Since a legitimate course had not been followed by the OAU, the Rabat government decided to withdraw from the Organisation in November 1984. The OAU was so disunited that it struggled even to hold a summit meeting and the divisive issue of Western Sahara never figured on its agenda again even after the OAU was renamed the African Union in July 2002. The issue was then moved to the United Nations where King Hassan II, in response to the UN Secretary General's appeal for a "search of a peaceful solution to the problem", offered, in October 1985, an immediate unilateral cease-fire on condition that the territories under his responsibility were not attacked. He also proposed the holding of a referendum under the auspices and control of the UN, in the early part of 1986.

A UN Peace plan was accepted by all parties on 30 August 1988 and a Settlement Plan was subsequently endorsed by the Security Council in June 1990, and the following year the UN brokered a cease-fire, which was implemented on 6 September 1991. The Settlement Plan included the holding of a UN-supervised referendum. An international peace-keeping force, MINURSO, was established in the area. The eligible voters were to decide whether they would prefer to be part of Morocco or opt for independence. MINURSO was empowered to compile a list of eligible voters who could vote in the referendum. The Spanish census of 1974 (less than 75,000) was used as a basis to start the identification process, but contrary to Polisario's claim, the census had not been completed by the Spanish administration. In 1995, the Identification Process broke down due to differences as to who should vote? What criteria to apply? And who should be able to identify the eligible voters? Most of the inhabitants of the Western Sahara had no fixed abode. In 1996, on the advice of the UN Secretary-General, the Security Council voted on 29 May 1996, to suspend the identification process.

In March, 1997 the UN Secretary-General, Kofi Annan, appointed former US Secretary of State, James Baker, to be his Personal Envoy with a remit to assess the feasibility of the UN Settlement Plan. During the year a series of talks led to the Houston Accords in September which "allowed for the resumption of the identification process".

In his report of June 2001 to the Security Council, the UN Secretary-General described the "serious difficulties encountered in carrying out and concluding the identification process" and went on to point out that the "appeals process promised to be even lengthier and more cumbersome and contentious than the identification process, which itself lasted for five and a half years". The process of identifying eligible voters ran into difficulties, partly because the UN relied mainly on Shioukhs (tribal leaders) from both sides to identify eligible voters for the referendum, and partly due to the fact that the inhabitants of the disputed territory did not have fixed abodes and had always followed a nomadic life-style. Furthermore, the tribal structure of the Sahrawis is very complex as is the rivalry between them. The Shioukhs accepted some voters and rejected others even when some potential voters came from the same family or tribe. Appeals from both sides ran to thousands of cases and the identification process was halted as it became quite clear it would turn into a nightmare for UN officials.

In view of these unexpected developments, the UN Secretary-General and his Personal Envoy, James Baker, concluded in 2000 that the Settlement Plan could not be implemented and that another approach must be sought. James Baker "reiterated that there were many ways to achieve self-determination". Security Council Resolution 1309 of 25 July 2000, called for an acceptable political solution. The UN proposed a Framework Agreement that would allow the Sahrawis the right to elect their own executive and legislative bodies, under Moroccan sovereignty, and have exclusive competence over a number of areas namely: local government administration, territorial budget and tax law enforcement, internal security, social welfare, culture, education, commerce, transportation, agriculture, mining, industry, fisheries, environmental policy, housing and urban development, water and electricity, and other basic infrastructure. This proposal was endorsed on 29 June, 2001 by the UN Security Council resolution 1359. Morocco accepted the proposal but Algeria and Polisario "expressed strong reservations" to the draft framework agreement and in November, the Algerian president, Abdelaziz Bouteflika, proposed another option: that of the partition of the territory. "It should also be noted that Algeria is described in the proposed plan as a neighbouring country, although it was referred to as a party to the dispute in the Secretary-General's report of 20 June, 2001 (S/2001/613) and the annexed Framework agreement".

The UN Secretary-General, Kofi Annan, pointed out in his report that "owing to the parties' incompatible positions with respect to the possibility of negotiating changes in the draft framework agreement, which was favoured by Morocco, or the proposal to divide the territory, which was favoured by Algeria and the Frente POLISARIO, I presented four options, which would not have required the concurrence of the parties, which the Security Council could consider in addressing the conflict over Western Sahara". The UN Secretary-General's four alternative solutions were the resumption of the UN settlement Plan, James Baker to revise the Framework Agreement, the partition of the territory or the termination of MINURSO by the UN Security Council.

In response to UN Security Council Resolution 1754 adopted in April 2007 asking the parties to negotiate without preconditions under UN auspices, four Manhasset meetings took place, near New York, in search for a political solution. Prior to the adoption of Resolution 1754 and the start of the ongoing UN-sponsored negotiations, Morocco had submitted a proposal to grant full autonomy to the Saharan region within the framework of the Kingdom's sovereignty and territorial integrity. The Polisario, however, had submitted their proposals a day before, insisting on the implementation of one of the options of the Baker Plan related to the holding of a referendum that the UN deemed unworkable because of the difficulties mentioned above.

The other choices under the Baker plan were autonomy or integration.

Under resolution 1359 (2001), The UN Secretary-General said that in order for the negotiations to take place, Algeria and the Polisario needed to express clearly their willingness to enter into them on the basis of the framework agreement as this was "the last window of opportunity for years to come". The first rounds of negotiations served as an icebreaker after years of hostility between the conflicting parties who reiterated their willingness to cooperate with the UN to break the stalemate. After mediating four rounds of talks and in his assessment of the situation on the ground, Peter van Walsum, the United Nations Secretary-General's special envoy and mediator in talks on Western

Sahara, told the UN Security Council that "an independent Western Sahara was not a realistic proposition". He continued: "My conclusion that an independent Western Sahara is not an attainable goal is relevant today because it lies at the root of the current negotiation process." Van Walsum added that "what matters is how political reality and international legality interact to enable us to take the best decisions in real life", and called on the Security Council to recommend to the parties involved in the dispute to resume negotiations and take into consideration the political and international realities. In a clear reference to the direct involvement of Algeria in the Sahara dispute, Ban Ki-moon's Personal Envoy blamed the persistence of the impasse on the fact that several countries deemed it "quite comfortable" to maintain the status-quo as it "spares them the responsibility of making difficult choices". He deplored the fact that the parties have not so far been able to engage in real negotiations and that "the process is deadlocked despite the agreement to hold a 5th round." He pointed out that "what is needed is a clearer advice from the Council itself. If the Council cannot make a choice, the parties cannot either."

Van Walsum suggested breaking the impasse by inviting the conflicting parties to reaffirm their principle of agreement that "nothing is agreed upon unless there is agreement on everything." He also recommended negotiations without preconditions "on the assumption that there will not be a referendum with independence as an option". He suggested that the UN Security Council should temporarily withdraw the two proposals from the negotiations agenda for six to nine months, stressing that the UN body "can affirm its intention to assess the process at the end of this trial period." "If it (UNSC) sees the outline of a possible political solution, it may decide to extend the trial period, otherwise the status-quo and the inconsistent stances of the parties will resume," he concluded.

In his report to the 15-member Security Council (S/2008/251) in April 2008, the UN Secretary-General Ban Ki-moon stated, "I concur with my Personal Envoy that the momentum can only be maintained by trying to find a way out of the current political impasse through realism and a spirit of compromise from both parties. The international community will share my view that the consolidation of the status quo is not an acceptable outcome of the current process of negotiations." UN Security Council Resolution 1813 called on the "the parties to continue to show political will and work in an atmosphere propitious for dialogue in order to enter into a more intensive and substantive phase of negotiations". A new UN envoy to the Western Sahara, the American diplomat Christopher Ross, was appointed in January 2009 and has embarked on a tour of the region to sound out prospects for resuming stalled talks between the conflicting parties.

After the UN-brokered cease-fire of 6 September 1991, it took Algeria and the Polisario fourteen years to release hundreds of prisoners of war some of whom had spent over twenty five years in holes in the ground, sometimes covered with corrugated iron, who were used as slave labour and several of them died in captivity on Algerian soil despite repeated calls for their release from the UN, the International Committee of the Red Cross and the UN High Commission for Refugees. The Sahrawis in the Tindouf Camps are confined to an Algerian military zone where no movement is allowed even for Algerian citizens without prior written authorisation from the Algerian military command. The Sahrawis in South-West Algeria have never been free to roam the desert which has been their natural habitat since time immemorial and their exact number is still unknown after more than three decades due to the fact that the Algerian authorities have consistently refused to allow the International Committee of the Red Cross or the UN High Commissioner for Refugees to conduct a census in the camps.

The Algerian military, the real power behind the regime since the country's independence in 1962, has been using the Sahrawis in the camps as pawns in a dangerous political game that could have dire consequences for the entire region if a political solution is not found in the near future. Morocco and Algeria have been locked into a longstanding dispute over the Sahara issue and only political will in Algiers and Rabat can solve it, said Boutros Ghali, former secretary-general of the UN in an interview with the Algerian Arabic daily "Al-Khabar". "Solving the Sahara issue lies in direct negotiations between Morocco and Algeria to reach a peaceful solution," he said.

If the Algerian leaders intend to solve the problem, it will not take long before North-West Africa rids itself of a protracted conflict that benefits no one and least of all the people of the region. Indeed, tangible talks between Morocco and Algeria are urgently needed and should be encouraged to pave the way for a peaceful settlement to a conflict that has lasted too long.

CHAPTER SEVEN: NATIONAL HUMAN DEVELOPMENT INITIATIVE (INDH)

In May 2005, King Mohammed VI launched the National Human Development Initiative (INDH) project as a major part of his plan to lift up the poor. The project is designed to improve inclusiveness, accountability and transparency of the decision-making and implementation processes at the local level so as to enhance the use of social and economic infrastructure and services by the poor and other vulnerable groups. The programme covers the alleviation of poverty in rural areas, the alleviation of social exclusion in urban areas, the alleviation of extreme vulnerability while also maintaining INDH governance mechanisms and strengthening of institutional capacity. By any standards this programme is ambitious and will demand a great deal of effort at many levels if it is to be fully and effectively implemented. A significant proportion of Morocco's population is poor and vulnerable. The World Bank has supported the initiative from the outset. INDH provides multi-sectoral public investments and income generating activities that target some 667 of Morocco's poorest neighbourhoods and rural communities. The programme follows a top-down approach in which local communities are enabled to express their needs and priorities in terms of basic infrastructure, social services and economic opportunities. Apart from $100 million loan to support the programme's implementation over the period 2007-10, the World Bank is also contributing to the INDH technical assistance and its worldwide experience in Community Driven Development (CDD) interventions. This support by the World Bank entails close collaboration with the INDH Steering Committee, the INDH Coordination Unit within the Ministry of the Interior, and the National Observatory of Human Development. World Bank initiatives in support of INDH are in line with its Country Assistance Strategy for Morocco, whose objective is to improve the lives of poor and marginalised groups. Any involvement by the World Bank means a series of steps before implementation can begin. In February 2006 an identification mission visited Morocco, in September an appraisal mission, and then in December the loan was approved. In June 2008 a study tour of Brazil was arranged for Moroccan officials and World Bank personnel working on the INDH project. In November there was a mission of evaluation followed by a Round Table of Walis and governors to study cases in December. In New York on 6 February 2009, Mohamed Loulichki, Morocco's ambassador to the UN, reiterated to the United Nations his country's commitment to build a modern society "based on rooting human rights culture" in order to achieve economic and social development. The INDH anti-poverty programme aims to curb all kinds of exclusion and spur human development in line with the UN Millennium Development Goals. The initiative required more than $1 billion over the period of 2006-10. Its principal objective is to help reduce unemployment and poverty in the most under privileged rural and urban communes. The Ambassador claimed that, "The Implementation of Morocco's 'Green Plan' would create tens of thousands of job opportunities and make the agricultural sector the main driving force of economic growth."

The plan is certainly ambitious. It puts social issues at the forefront of political priorities and its most positive feature is its participatory approach involving civil society and local authorities in the planning and implementation. However, it is less clear how the INDH fits in with the national development strategy or the general economic policy. There is also the question as to whether it will assist in the transfer of greater political power and resources to local governments to make them key agents in the democracy building process. When King Mohammed VI launched the INDH project he pointed out that social problems were "the main challenge we must face to achieve our project for society and development." Segments of Morocco's population and entire areas of the country live in conditions of poverty and marginalisation incompatible with a dignified and decent life.

In his speech, King Mohammed VI assumed the state's responsibility to undertake 'social modernisation' by means of integrated public policies. The focal points of the INDH are to reduce social deficit by basic infrastructure and social services, to promote income generating activities and employment and to offer assistance to the most vulnerable social groups. Since complete coverage of all vulnerable groups was not possible, 360 rural municipalities and 250 marginal neighbourhoods or old quarters were designated as priority beneficiaries of the programme. Through 2005 the institutional arrangements to launch the INDH were designed and the first 1104 projects for priority action were selected. There was a total budget of Dh250m (euro23m). The resources allocated for 2005 came from the national budget (Dh50m) ($6m) and (Dh100m) ($12m) from local authorities and the Hassan II Fund for Economic and Social Development. For the period 2006-2010, it was estimated that local authorities and international aid would each provide 20 per cent of required funds while the government would provide 60 per cent. The INDH reflects the desire on the part of the monarchy to make social development a priority. As the King said: "Any exploitation of social misery for political purposes or to feed extremist fervour or to nurture a feeling of pessimism, defeatism or desperation, is morally unacceptable."

The INDH purposefully adopts a human development perspective and philosophy, and puts an end to what the Fiftieth Anniversary Report (of independence) calls a policy of growth without development. The most positive aspect of INDH is its participatory approach and integration of different agents in a single process. There is also relative transparency in the selection of priorities and projects. In the long run the INDH should be about bottom up development rather than top down. To be eligible projects must generate income, improve access to basic services, involve social and cultural activities or strengthen local capacities and governance. All this is very positive but there are some difficult questions to be faced. First, how does the INDH programme fit in with the country's overall development strategy? The resources available for the INDH programme are insufficient for an initiative that is designed to tackle Morocco's social problems. The task facing the implementation of the INDH programme is very challenging and commendable if it yields results. Although statistically Morocco is a middle income country (GDP per capita $2,200 in 2008), its social indicators are those of a less developed country. For the INDH to succeed, it will require a greater proportion of the country's resources than it is allocated at present and it should be fully integrated into the national development strategy. The management and implementation of INDH has been given to provincial governors who are responsible to the Ministry of the Interior, although the Prime Minister oversees strategic supervision at the national level. The INDH should certainly lead to tangible results in the short term and these can easily be monitored and evaluated. The big question is whether they will become part of a long-term development process and whether INDH projects will expand people's choices. In his speech, the King called for the government to "take steps to listen to and work together with all active players in the country, including political parties, trade unions, local groups, civil society organisations and the private sector" and that means a great deal of cooperation between different groups that will often be pursuing different policies. In the long run, the success of the INDH will depend largely upon the extent of the goodwill of all parties concerned and interested.

In 2009, four years after the launch of the INDH, 16,000 projects costing more than 9.4 billion Dhs ($1.2 billion) had been initiated and more than four million citizens had benefited from these projects. On the fourth anniversary of the launching of INDH, some notable progress had been made in the business of ameliorating conditions of life for the poorest and the numbers of the very poor had been reduced from 14 per cent to 9 per cent of the population. The INDH projects had become a reality for many living on the fringes of society in different regions of the country. The emphasis of the programme has been on social mobilisation based upon participation and inclusion and the development of a culture of transparency and reinforcing a sense of citizenship and belonging to the nation. Thus, 11,000 men and women had been enrolled in groups in the different prefectures of the country. The fourth anniversary of INDH was celebrated during May 2009 in Fez, Dakhla, Marrakech and Rabat.

The INDH project aims to ally ambition, realism and efficacy. It includes the participation of the elected representatives, heads of ministerial departments, experts from ministries and components of civil society and the private sector all of whom have taken part. INDH has coordinated the efforts of different parties and given a fresh impetus, especially to women and young people in order to strengthen their contribution to a re-launch of human capital. The plan of action of INDH is fixed upon good governance that in particular aims to revitalise a sense of responsibility and transparency among different social actors.

CHAPTER EIGHT: HUMAN RIGHTS

As soon as he came to the throne, King Mohammed VI pushed through the reform of the Mudawana, which had been initiated by his father a few months before his death. There was fierce opposition to the reform of the family code by Islamist groups, prominent among them is "Al Adl Wal Ihsan" organising massive demonstrations against it in Casablanca. The reform eventually became law in February 2004. The new code introduced major changes that favoured the position of women. It raised the marriage age from 15 to 18, allowed women to divorce by mutual consent, curbed the right of men to ask for divorce unilaterally, restricted the practice of polygamy and replaced the wife's duty of obedience with the concept of joint responsibility. Problems of implementation, both deliberate and circumstantial, followed. These included judges untrained in administering the new code or lack of information among women as to what were their rights yet despite these immediate limitations upon performance the reform placed Morocco in the forefront of Arab and Muslim states over the issue of women's rights. In the first year of King Mohammed's reign, encouraged by his progressive outlook, civil society began to play a more important role in politics and pressed for further reforms. These concerned compensation for the victims of past repression and the bringing to trial of those responsible. Sections of the press pushed for further reforms to test how free the press could become.

During King Hassan's reign, thousands of Moroccans had been illegally detained, imprisoned, sometimes tortured, or forcibly "disappeared" by state action. In April 2004 King Mohammed VI formally established the first truth-seeking body in the Middle East and North Africa and a 17-member Commission was charged with investigating the former era and providing compensation to victims and their families. A human rights activist and leader, Driss Benzekri, who had spent 17 years as a political prisoner in one of Morocco's secret detention centres, was appointed Commission President by the King. At this time the King pardoned 27 prisoners who were released. In December 2004, the Commission began public hearings which were broadcast live on radio and television, including on Al Jazeera, and nothing like this had occurred before in the Arab world, while victims of serious abuses over the years 1956-1999 described their experiences. Over eighteen months, the Commission received more than 22,000 applications for consideration and held victim-centred public hearings that were televised throughout the country. The Equity and Reconciliation Commission (IER) presented its final report to the palace on 30 November 2005 and two weeks later, the King mandated the public dissemination of the several hundred-page report, to mark a crucial moment in Moroccan history. Determining the responsibility of state and other actors for the abuses and outlining an extensive reparations plan for victims and their families, the report set out concrete recommendations which included substantial institutional and legislative reforms that would provide Morocco with a momentous opportunity to advance victims' rights and prevent further abuses. From December 2003, the ICTJ worked closely with the IER, providing ongoing technical assistance and advice while also actively engaging with Moroccan human rights organisations, the media, and victims' groups to stress their role in monitoring the Commission and assisting victims.

In May 2007, Driss Benzekri died after a short illness and was greatly mourned. Benzekri had first hand experience of these human rights abuses. He had been jailed and tortured in 1974 for Marxist activism while a student and remained a prisoner for 17 years. On his release, he began to uncover the truth about those who had been subjected to similar treatment. He found that many officials and security personnel maintained a wall of silence for fear of retribution. The situation only began to change in 1999 after the accession of Mohammed VI. The new King pledged greater openness about the country's painful past and promised greater tolerance for dissent. In 2000, Benzekri was approached on behalf of the King and asked to help in addressing the grievances of those who had suffered at the hands of the state. He agreed and his mandate, as head of the IER, had been to lift the veil of secrecy over the political abuses that had occurred during the previous reign. His death provided an opportunity to assess the process of rehabilitation. Human rights activists, for example, complained that the Commission did not have the power to bring charges against those responsible for the human rights violations that had taken place although a number of police and prison administrators had been arrested on charges of using torture and were to face prosecution. The Commission had determined that 300 people had been shot dead during demonstrations, that almost 200 had died after arbitrary detention and more than 9,000 had suffered abuses – wrongful imprisonment and torture. Benzekri's leadership of the Commission had been all the more remarkable and challenging due to his chronic back pain, the result of torture, and the stomach cancer that led to his death. His aim was truth rather than revenge. The government showed a good deal of courage and determination in dealing with the issue of former abuses since the Commission had many enemies in high places because it stood for the rejection of the system they had established and run. The King showed considerable personal bravery in setting up the Commission since the abuses under investigation had occurred during the reign of his father, Hassan II. In an official reaction to Benzekri's death, the King praised the former dissident for his courage and integrity.

It is far from easy to assess the full impact of any exercise in restitution, reconciliation or rehabilitation. Shortly after his accession to the throne, King Mohammed VI released a large number of political prisoners including Abdessalam Yassine, the leader of the largest Islamist movement, Al Adl wal Ihsan, who was released from house arrest although he was responsible for scathing attacks upon both Hassan II and Mohammed VI. He also gave permission in September 1999 for the dissident Abraham Serfaty to return to Morocco from exile in France. The King strengthened the *Conseil Consultatif des Droits de l'Homme* (CCDH) (Human Rights Consultative Council) by appointing Ahmed Herzenni, a former opposition political activist and prisoner, in charge of its affairs although its subsequent annual reports appeared too restrained to international human rights organisations. The King brought Moroccan laws further into line with international conventions including the abolition of torture. Most important, Mohammed VI acknowledged the government's responsibility for the forced disappearances and other former abuses of human rights. He did so less than a month after his accession and then announced the formation of an Independent Arbitration Panel to review individual cases and compensate victims. This first panel was disbanded in 2003 although by then it had paid compensation to 4,000 victims. However, a few months later the King established the *Instance Equite et Reconciliation* (IER), referred to above. It is important to consider whether these two Commissions succeeded in putting to rest the many claims of human rights abuses. The Independent Arbitration Panel, for example, set a very short deadline for applications and so cut off thousands of people who might have come forward while it paid monetary damage to victims and their families without raising the issue of reconciliation. The scope of the IER was broader and it aimed more at uncovering truth and encouraging reconciliation than only providing financial compensation. On the other hand it had no authority to compel testimony from the security services while its mandate only extended to 1999. Despite criticisms, the IER was an unprecedented initiative in the Arab world: it interviewed thousands of victims, conducted investigations throughout Morocco, held public hearings (often on television, radio or the Internet) and built up a data base of 22,000 personal testimonies. More important, it emphasised the responsibility of the government for human rights abuses.

Morocco claims a tolerance that is not to be found in other Arab states and the unanimous adoption at the beginning of 2004 by both Chambers of Parliament of the bill, which incorporated the new family code that emphasised the equality of the sexes, clearly represented a major advance. The King had issued strict instructions to Parliament that the basic principles incorporated in the new code must not be changed. This legislation was considered to be the most important reform since the King's accession and was also seen to be the most progressive law on women's and family rights in the Arab world. However, though the King insisted that the new code should be implemented effectively, it was acknowledged that there would be problems enforcing it.

On 18 January 2007, the cabinet officially adopted an amendment to the nationality code to allow Moroccan women married to foreigners to pass on citizenship to their children. Doubts at this amendment were expressed but it was passed by Parliament and appeared in the official bulletin on April 2. Implementation presented some problems since the issuing of identity cards was subject to obstruction by local officials who objected to the new rules. However, it was a triumph for liberals who had championed the new law. According to human rights groups many women workers are exploited, particularly in the textile industry. The government has promised tighter supervision although the problem is essentially one of attitudes. In any case, the government is reluctant to exert too much pressure on firms that provide thousands of jobs for the country's poorest citizens. Women's rights organisations believe education is the real key to progress. Illiteracy among women stands at 80 per cent and this acts as a major impediment to their awareness of their rights and their employment options. The King has concentrated upon providing new educational opportunities in rural areas and campaigns are being mounted to change traditional attitudes that persuade families to neglect the education of girls. Adult literacy programmes are being expanded and foreign non-governmental organisations (NGOs) working in this field are being encouraged.

Thirty-five women were elected to parliament in 2002 and this figure altered only marginally in 2007 when 34 women were elected, just over 10 per cent of the legislature seats and only just above the 10 per cent reserved for women. Changing attitudes are just as important as new laws. A National Survey on Values of 2004 found that 60 per cent of Moroccans believed that men made better leaders than women although 82.2 per cent said they were willing to support female candidates. One woman MP, Nouzha Skalli, argued that because so many men vote for members of their own gender, women should do the same. Lower down the scale of job opportunities quotas are still uncommon so that women only occupy 10 per cent or less of local council seats. Thus, gender equality still has a long way to go and there will be many tussles and setbacks before full equality is achieved but the fact that the subject is now openly debated represents a major advance in the face of longstanding traditions about the place of women in society.

In 2009, both the government and women's groups were still working to convince a conservative society to change with the times. According to Nouzha Skalli, the minister of social development, family and solidarity, "the new law has done a lot towards gender equality, but it's not a magic wand. For centuries women have been considered as fit only for marriage and submission to their husbands – a law can't transform that overnight." Historically, Morocco has followed Islamic customs regarding the family. These allowed fathers to give their daughters in marriage, and granted them only half the share of inheritance than their male offsprings. Males were allowed to take up to four wives simultaneously and divorce them at will. The first family law, passed after Morocco gained independence from France in 1956, did little except codify existing practices. Significant change only came in 2004, when King Mohammed VI pushed through the new family code "the Mudawwana". Although the reforms have not been welcomed by traditional Moroccans who see them as a breach of Islamic law, they are in accordance with the growing independence of women.

Despite these changes, however, male dominance remains entrenched. As Rhizlane Benachir, president of the Association Jousour "bridges" (a Rabat-based charity that seeks to combat widespread illiteracy that keeps some women trapped in their homes and ignorant of their rights), claims, "Women who can't read and write are dependent on a father or husband. In that sense, they remain like children all their lives. We are teaching them to become citizens." At the same time, the public schools are teaching them about women's rights, and imams talk about the issue in Morocco's state-controlled mosques". Mrs Benradi of Mohammed V University in Rabat says, "today, the majority of women want financial independence, and many couples need two incomes to get by. But the men have grown up in an environment in which they have all the power." Economic development as well as laws will hasten changes in attitudes towards women. Prosperity will create a middle-class where husband and wife will need two incomes and the wife's capacity to earn a second income should help to break down the old traditions.

Women now have jobs in all sectors of the economy, according to a Guide to Morocco. There are women ministers, royal advisers, governors, political delegates, ambassadors, airline pilots, company directors, Olympic champions, policemen, soldiers, train drivers, writers, publishers, active militants and journalists. These advances began in 1972 when an amendment to the constitution granted women the right to vote and be elected. In 1994, 77 women were elected to the Chamber of Representatives. However, feminist associations were not satisfied with these advances and demanded the abolition of the family code (Mudawwana) as it had been enacted in 1957, just after independence from France. Moves to raise the status of women in March 1999 (shortly before Hassan II died) met with bitter resistance. The proposed changes were opposed by the Minister of Religious Affairs, the ulemas (councils) and parliament's Islamic deputies and were only finally passed into law in 2004. However, the struggle for women's equality still has a long way to go. Some Islamists as well as secular conservatives argue that the extension of greater rights to women was a mistake because it broke with tradition and threatened to weaken family bonds. On the other side, liberals of different persuasions claim that the rate of women's emancipation is too slow. Nonetheless, more and more women were taking on responsible positions and, for example, following the 2007 elections five women were appointed ministers and two secretaries of state in the new government. Women headed the ministries of Energy, Mines, Water, the Environment, Health, Youth and Sport.

The more public discussion that takes place, the more open a society becomes. In July 2006, for example, an international conference, "Media Advisory: Reflective Conference on Transitional Justice in Morocco", was held and discussed transitional justice, human rights, and the lessons learned from the Moroccan Truth-seeking Experience. The occasion featured panel discussions with former commissioners, representatives of Moroccan NGOs, ministers and political leaders. The result of the reforms, even if they are often ignored or not adequately implemented, nonetheless has made Morocco a more open society and ensured that the issues are publicly debated. Civil society organisations focus on human rights and women's rights while women's organisations have come to play a crucial role in building up support for the reformed Mudawwana family code. NGOs have found that they are successful when they work with the government rather than against it. They will not be able to force the government to initiate reforms it does not want although by constant pressure they may be able to prevent backsliding. Critics of the reform process point to corruption and the difficulty in practice of people obtaining justice according to the new laws but as a Middle East Report of 2009 says, "give time a chance". The King's tasks are not easy. "Mohammed VI has no reliable institutional partners with whom to pursue necessary political reforms, and he faces two formidable adversaries if he attempts to lead the democratisation and modernisation fights alone. These are the Islamists and the old establishment, which is opposed to radical changes.

In March 2009 the Secretary General of Amnesty International, Irene Khan, visited Rabat. She congratulated the Moroccan authorities on progress made on human rights but called for urgent action on a range of major concerns. Meeting with Justice Minister Abdelwahed Radi and Interior Minister Chakib Benmoussa, Khan noted the positive steps taken on women's rights but went on to say: " government must now consolidate the progress by criminalizing violence against women, which has long been a demand of Moroccan women's rights. While acknowledging that the establishment of the Equity and Reconciliation Commission was the first of its kind in the Arab world, Khan expressed concern that three years later, many of its recommendations had yet to be implemented and she urged the government promptly to ratify the

International Convention on Enforced Disappearances."

Khan also urged the authorities to respect the right to the peaceful expression of political opinion. On the positive side, Amnesty International noted that Morocco had not carried out any executions since 1993. "Morocco can be a role model in the region by instituting a moratorium on the death penalty. The Moroccan authorities should join the majority of the world that no longer carries out capital punishment."

According to the Middle East Report of February 2009 (already quoted), the reforming King has two adversaries. First are the Islamists "who resist any modern alternative to the existing authoritarian system even as they chastise its social ills. The King's less obvious and more dangerous adversaries are the entrenched interests within the administration, the public sector, the military and the security apparatus. These groups benefit the most from the perpetuation of authoritarian rule." Reform in a conservative society is never easy. Morocco under King Mohammed VI has made great strides in the last ten years yet, apart from deliberate foot-dragging by officials in the implementation of reforms that have already been passed into law, there are still many areas that remain to be tackled.

Hassan II Mosque in Casablanca

The King inaugurating the Oujda industrial zone

Amir Al Muminun (Commander of the Faithful)

CHAPTER NINE: ISLAM AND TERRORISM

Turmoil in the Islamic world, in part a response to the West as in Afghanistan, Iraq or Pakistan, and in part an internal struggle between Islamist and secular forces as in Morocco's neighbour Algeria, has as its instrument the terrorist. King Mohammed VI has stated his determination to reform and modernise the state he rules but to succeed he must take account of the old established centres of power on the one hand and the Islamist extremists who would stop or reverse his reforms on the other. A majority of Moroccans do not trust the old political parties, which they see as sterile and corrupt, and fear the Islamist extremists. As moderates they are quite capable of separating their religious duty from their civil rights. They want reforms that will improve their lives. The Islamists oppose reforms that would confine religion to the private sphere while the secular authorities would enforce the rule of law in all other matters. Morocco still requires huge changes to bring it into the modern world and lift the majority of its people out of poverty, and the King faces a dilemma since as Commander of the Faithful he must act as the protector of private religious rights and as the secular executive ruler of the country he must guarantee civil rights and any new reforms that he initiates.

Morocco is a moderate and reasonably stable society. The King is also Commander of the Faithful, which imposes a double burden upon him but evades the problem faced by Iran where a spiritual leader and a political leader vie for power. There are three necessities for people that Islam has to protect: their life, their wealth and their dignity as people. The question is whether Islam can fulfill this role alongside the government or in opposition to it. Poor people are conservative and the King has made a point of moving amongst them – the guardian of the poor – to ensure that they do not become prey to Islamist extremists acting as their champions. As Commander of the Faithful, the King has the final religious word but that does not mean his reforms will not be challenged by extremists or conservative reactionaries. The state faces the need to educate people to a degree of tolerance in relation to the world in which Morocco operates and religion, which used to be a matter for the community, needs more and more support from the state. On the other hand, there is need for tolerance: Muslims are forbidden to drink or sell alcohol but if they do it is a matter for their conscience and God and not for the state. There should be no compulsion to Islam; rather, it belongs to the individual to choose. All peoples should accept each other's religions. Such a tolerant approach to religion is rejected by Islamist extremists.

Morocco's neighbour Algeria was wracked by a brutal civil war between secularists and Islamists through the last decade of the 20th century and into the present century and there is an abiding fear in Rabat that terrorist extremism will spread across the border. The terrorist outrages in Casablanca in May 2003 acted as the catalyst for an intensified security policy in Morocco. On 16 May 2003 suicide bombers in Casablanca exploded at least five bombs that targeted a Spanish restaurant, a five star hotel, a Jewish Community Centre and the Belgian consulate to kill 45 people, including 12 bombers, while injuring a further 60 people. Subsequently some 2,000 people were arrested in connection with the bombings, according to Mohamed Bouzoubaa, the Justice Minister. Thirty international arrest warrants were also issued. Speaking to the French newspaper *Le Figaro*, the head of Morocco's security services, General Hamidou Laanigri, said, "As far as I know; only a dozen dangerous elements are still at large. Of course, attacks are still possible. We are not completely safe, even if the cleaning up operation is well under way." Ten days after the bombings the British *Sunday Telegraph* claimed that Abu Qatada, the Muslim cleric then held in Britain, was linked to the Casablanca suicide bombings. Moroccan investigators found material from his sermons in the homes of the suicide bombers. The sermons praise Osama bin Laden and encourage young Muslims to take a stand against the West. This Casablanca tragedy led to a significant tightening of security measures in Morocco.

In 2005, the King pardoned 285 Islamists who had been condemned under anti-terrorist legislation and commuted the death penalty imposed upon another 24. On 11 March 2007, a man detonated explosives under his clothes at an internet café in Casablanca to kill himself and wound three others. It was the first such incident since 2003 when 45 people had been killed in Casablanca. A few days later the police arrested 18 people in connection with the internet suicide bomb attack and a spokesman said six other suspects remained at large. According to officials the Mehdi group from which the man came was planning an even bigger attack and had recruited members of the police and the military. The case of those subsequently brought to trial was seen by foreign diplomats and human rights activists as a test for the government's pledges to balance its fight against radical Islamists with respect for human rights. Security officials claimed that the police had broken up more than 50 radical Islamist cells, some of which were linked to Al Qaida, and had arrested more than 3,000 people since the 2003 bombings in Casablanca. Local human rights groups accused the authorities of abusing the rights of arrested people many of whom, they argued, had been detained on unfounded suspicion of links to terrorism. The government denied that any abuses had taken place and said that anti-terrorism trials in Morocco were fair and respected the rights of defendants. One theory about the March bomb was that the man was trying to access websites, or make e-mail contact to receive instructions on where to detonate the explosives. Several of those arrested were said to be linked to a series of coordinated suicide bombings in 2003. Intelligence experts claimed that terrorists were operating in Europe and Morocco, travelling on false passports. One man was seen as a Morocco-Spain-London link. Jamal Zougan was born in Morocco in 1973 in Tangier and moved with his mother to Spain in 1983. With two others he was later implicated in the Madrid bombing. Also in March 2007 chaos erupted at the trial of 50 Moroccan Islamists accused of plotting to overthrow the monarchy after they began to hurl abuse at the judge for delaying their hearing a third time. Some of the men climbed onto a glass wall separating them from the public section of the courtroom, shouting that the trial was a charade and the accusations against them trumped up to please Morocco's staunch ally the United States. The accused were charged with belonging to the militant Ansar el Mehdi (Mehdi Partisans), undermining public order and collecting money to fund terrorist attacks. The prosecution said the group wanted to overthrow the monarchy that had ruled Morocco for almost five centuries and replace it with an Islamist state. If convicted they would face up to 30 years in prison. The government claimed that the capture of the group proved the existence of an increasingly sophisticated menace to the stability and security of the country.

In April 2007 a suicide bomber blew themselves up in Casablanca close to the city's US consulate and American cultural centre. The Al Jazeera correspondent in Morocco said the police were searching for a second suspect who had fled the scene following the blasts. Earlier that week three men had detonated explosive belts in Casablanca and police shot and killed a fourth man who appeared to be preparing to detonate explosives. The police had been pursuing the men in connection with the explosion at the internet café on 11 March. A senior police officer told Reuters, "there is no doubt they aimed at US targets. They made that statement with their own bodies." Other witnesses said that one man approached the US consulate and the other the cultural centre before blowing themselves up one minute apart. An internet statement, apparently from Al Qaida, claimed responsibility for the bombings but the government in Rabat insisted that the bombers were "home grown" with no links to international groups. The police said they were hunting for about 10 more possible suicide bombers. The BBC's Richard Hamilton in Rabat said a dawn police chase across the rooftops of the poor El Fida district in Casablanca ended when two men were cornered. One detonated his belt of explosives and killed himself, the other was shot by police. Later that day a third man was found who blew himself up; a police officer died of his injuries and a seven-year old child was hurt. These incidents followed the death of their "alleged" leader who had blown himself up in the internet café in March. Another bomb, which killed the bomber and injured four others including a suspected accomplice, was condemned by the Prime Minister, Driss Jettou, who said the attacks "would not affect Morocco's efforts towards consolidating its democratic process." The blast occurred on a Sunday evening in the district of Sidi Moumen, Casablanca's largest slum. The bomber and his accomplice had not targeted the internet café but had an argument with the owner over access to the internet.

In July, Hassan Khattab, a Moroccan Islamist charged with leading a cell that plotted to overthrow the country's monarchy claimed that he only knew a handful of the 49 other suspected members in the courtroom in Sale near the capital Rabat. The government claimed that the capture of the Ansar el Mehdi group proved the existence of an increasingly sophisticated menace to the Kingdom. The mass trial had faced numerous delays because the judge rejected the requests by some of the accused to defend themselves and defence lawyers complained about cameras in the courtroom.

The 50 accused were finally convicted and sentenced to various prison terms in January 2008. The alleged mastermind, Hassan al-

Khattab was given a 25-year sentence while the other 49, including four women and several members of the security forces, received sentences of two to 10 years. Meanwhile, early in July, the Interior Ministry had raised its security alert level to the highest rating of "maximum", suggesting an attack by Al Qaida-linked radical Islamists was imminent. Human rights groups implied anti-terrorist overkill when they accused the authorities of abusing the rights of arrested people. Many, they argued, were detained on unfounded suspicion of links to terrorism. The government denied any abuses and claimed that anti-terrorism trials were fair and respected the rights of defendants. What had become plain by 2007 was the extent of the terrorist threat. The bomb attacks of May 2003 in Casablanca were not a one-off outrage but had ushered in a new period of heightened tension.

The US State Department produces country reports on terrorism and its 2008 report on Morocco, published in April 2009, provides a detailed analysis of government policy. The report opens with the following statement: "Morocco pursued a comprehensive counter-terrorism approach that emphasized vigilant security measures, including international cooperation, and counter-radicalisation policies." It suggested that the threat of terrorist attacks stemmed from the existence of numerous small "grassroots" extremist groups. They remained isolated from one another, were small in size and tactically limited. The existence of these relatively small groups pointed to the need for continued vigilance. The government's counter-terrorism efforts have done a good job in minimising the threat but the fact that small groups appear, unrelated to each other, would suggest that there is a relatively widespread jihadist movement that is unlikely to disappear and could become much more dangerous if these groups begin to make contact with one another. Considerable numbers of Moroccans are reported to have gone to northern Mali and Algeria to receive training from Al Qaida though, so far, Al Qaida has not mounted any successful terrorist attacks in Morocco although it may have influenced extremists through website propaganda. The government is concerned about the number of Moroccans returning from Iraq where they have learnt terrorist tactics. The Moroccan government has adopted a counter-terrorism approach that builds upon the popular rejection of terrorism and searches and eliminates terrorist cells through traditional law enforcement and pre-emptive security measures. King Mohammed VI has promoted efforts to reduce extremism while information provided by ordinary citizens has assisted the security authorities in detecting terrorist groups. Following the Casablanca bombings of 2003, the government has focused on upgrading places of worship, modernising the teaching of Islam and strengthening the Ministry of Endowments and Islamic Affairs. The Council of Ulamas, Morocco's highest religious body, was charged by the King, who is its leader, to "combat the hoaxes peddled by proponents of extremism," and to ensure the safeguarding of Morocco's tolerant Sunni Islam identity. In September 2008, the King announced a "proximity strategy" and called for the rehabilitation of 3,180 mosques, the training of 33,000 imams and an increase of Ulama council members from 30 to 70 across the country to propagate a culture of religious tolerance and confront extremism. The perceived injustice suffered by the Palestinian people has been cited by Moroccan officials as the single greatest radicalising element among Moroccan extremists. Social reforms and the elimination of poverty are vital elements in fighting extremism and the National Initiative for Human Development (NIHD), which was launched in 2005, is a $1.2 billion programme to generate employment and combat poverty with special focus upon rural areas. An anti-money laundering bill passed in 2007 was implemented in 2008. It provides for the freezing of suspicious accounts and allows for the prosecution of terrorist finance related crimes. Moroccan police, customs, central bank and financial officials are receiving training from the US and the EU. The government has made plain its commitment not to use the struggle against terrorism to deprive individuals of their rights and has emphasised its adherence to human rights standards. In November 2008, the government announced a $27.5 million programme to improve prison conditions and alleviate overcrowding. Part of the government strategy is to make new and existing penitentiary space available for re-education and social reintegration into society. Rehabilitaion and training prorammes have also been introduced in prisons to allow detainees to come out with skills allowing them to find jobs and reintegrate society easily and not be marginalised and regarded as outcast as was the case in the past.

Morocco has extended its counter terrorism activities to increased international cooperation, disrupting potential attacks upon foreign, Western targets and investigating individuals associated with international terrorist groups. Sharing information and joint operations with African, Arab or European security services is now part of its anti-terrorist strategy. Although Morocco has experienced less terrorist activity than some other countries, it has become plain since 2003 that Islamist terrorism and subversion are now an ongoing and potentially destabilising factor in the country's life. In response, the government is increasing its security branches and training while also tackling problems of poverty and deprivation, which can so easily become breeding grounds for discontent.

Al -Karaouine University in Fez, the oldest university in the world

CHAPTER TEN: MEDIA AND FREEDOM OF EXPRESSION

The freedom of the press is one of the essential principles of democracy and one of the indispensable foundations for the setting up of a credible democratic system. It is also one of the paramount conditions for the implementation of the rule of law in a liberal, multi-party system, with different doctrines and divergent political and ideological tendencies.

Following his succession to his father, King Mohammed VI raised the hope of a radical reform of Moroccan press laws. He counteracted his father's strict rule by allowing two weekly magazines, *"Le Journal Hebdomadaire"* and *"Demain Magazine"*, previously banned, to be republished in January 2001. Furthermore, some journalists, who were critical of King Hassan II's rule and went into exile or were imprisoned, were released and allowed to return to the country. He also instigated reforms to the Press Code and broadcasting in conjunction with his plans for full-fledged democracy. Article 9 of the 1996 Moroccan Constitution provides that "the Constitution shall guarantee all citizens the following: (b) freedom of opinion, expression in all its forms, and public gathering." The same article adds, however: "No limitation, except by law, shall be put to the exercise of such freedoms." It is this exception that allowed the Moroccan legislature to adopt an array of laws limiting freedom of expression.

In a speech on Coronation Day, 30 July 2005, the King highlighted his intentions in this regard, asserting that "we have managed to introduce decisive institutional and political reforms, which have created new momentum and given substance to democratic practice in our country. Today, we want the normal exercise of democracy to be deeply-rooted in our society".

The Parliamentary Commission for Foreign Affairs and National Defence adopted a new national press code on February 8, 2002. Somewhat more lenient than its predecessor and containing fewer criminal penalties for libel, the code nonetheless still maintains sentences of three to five years imprisonment for defaming the King or the royal family, as compared with five to twenty years imprisonment in the previous code. Article 29 also gives the government the right to shut down any publication "prejudicial to Islam, the monarchy, territorial integrity, or public order." Despite the liberal licensing system in the Press Law, it still provides sanctions against any criticism of "sacred" issues. The Press Law also protects various public institutions and foreign heads of state against defamation and restricts reporting on cases under judicial deliberation.

Moroccan officials maintain that the kingdom enjoys a freedom of the press unparalleled in other Arab or African nations. It is a fact that Morocco has never silenced political criticism in the press with the ruthlessness and violence evidenced in Africa and the Arab world. As the King pointed out in an interview with the international Arabic daily "Asharq al-Awsat" in July 2001: "Of course I am for press freedom, but I would like that freedom to be responsible....I personally appreciate the critical role that the press and Moroccan journalists play in public debate, but we need to be careful not to give in to the temptation of the imported model. The risk is seeing our own values alienated.... There are limits set by the law".

A Media Sustainability Index (MSI) panel viewed 2005 as a year when many free-speech taboos were broken—provoking new calls from the government for respect to be shown to journalism ethics. For their part, media professionals sought adoption by the government of a law that guarantees the right to access public information and the abolition of prison sentences for defamation. While the Moroccan government accepts political criticism it does not tolerate any attack on the monarchy or Islam. Journalists and newspaper editors are considered professionals who must report the news, but they are also considered educated, patriotic citizens who should be mindful of their social responsibilities to the public. To guarantee that criticism of official policies remains within appropriate bounds, the government grants a subsidy of 50 million Dirhams to the press ($6.5 million) each year. Since advertising revenues and newsstand sales represent only a slim portion of the operating budget of most Moroccan newspapers, the yearly government subsidy provides welcome financial assistance but at the same time acts as a useful brake that prevents some Moroccan publications from operating with full autonomy and independence. In theory, the subsidy is provided to encourage and promote an independent press with high professional standards. By western norms, however, the very existence of such subsidies is difficult to reconcile with the establishment of an autonomous free press.

As a former French protectorate, Morocco enjoys the diversity of a bilingual press. Newspapers are published either in French or Arabic. The French language is used by the Moroccan elite who send their children to French schools. These are still believed to provide a better grounding for potential employment and openings for a wider range of professional careers. On the other hand, Arabic, the official language, remains the spoken language of the masses but since the 1970s, has become more widely used. Arabic-language newspapers have flourished and now represent the majority of the Moroccan press partly because Morocco has been consciously reclaiming its cultural heritage. Even the elite have started to acknowledge the national and international usefulness of the Arabic language especially in the political sphere in the same way that English has been adopted for business and finance.

The print media market is open to any Moroccan investor, but foreigners are barred by law from investing in publications registered in Morocco. Foreign investors can set up their own publications under different regulations, one of which requires prior authorization from the Ministry of Communication and the publication of a decree in the official bulletin. The conditions imposed on Moroccan publications are liberal, and rarely is a registration request denied. The political liberalization in Morocco is translated into a simple request from the district attorney, who authenticates the application documents, for anyone intending to publish a newspaper or a magazine. The state deals with publications as it deals with any other kind of company without distinction or privilege.

In the past, the majority of Moroccan newspapers did not represent viable commercial ventures or profit-making corporations, partly because they were essentially the mouthpieces of political parties. As such they were owned by political interests and survived on contributions and government subsidies. In recent years, however, an influx of new capital has led to the creation of newspapers and periodicals that aspire to become commercially profitable and enjoy financial autonomy and editorial independence. These new publications have introduced a new dimension into press coverage in the country, revitalized investigative journalism and broken new ground into what previously were considered taboo subjects. These publications have nourished a new generation of journalists who are keen to report anything of interest to readers and Moroccan society at large and are bent on getting their way even at the cost of going to prison. The country's most assertive political publications are those willing to scrutinize the activities of powerful personalities, track corruption, and tackle sensitive political issues.

Some journalists have experienced clashes with the authorities, with political personalities, with influential economic operators, the judiciary and even with the royal family. They have been taken to court for libel and some have been heavily fined and given suspended prison sentences. The growing role of the press in the democratic process that is now taking place in the country has led to increasing debate. A national forum on the print media was held in March 2005 to examine problems facing the media and discuss obstacles and material problems that face journalists and publishers in the performance of their professional duties. As a result, a contract was signed between the Ministry of Communication, the Federation of Moroccan newspaper publishers (*Fédération Marocaine des Editeurs de journaux*, FMEJ) and the National Union of the Moroccan Press (*le Syndicat National de la Presse Marocaine*, SNPM) aimed at assisting in the development of the media through funding, training, and management support. The contract also allows for the modernisation of the print media to achieve "a free and professional journalistic practice in the context of the rule of law".

In addition, the Ministry, the Association of Advertisers and the Federation of Newspaper Publishers approved an accord establishing the first office responsible for measuring the circulation of newspapers "OJD" (Office de Justification de la Diffusion). The year also witnessed a series of consultations by the Ministry of Communication with political parties and media professionals regarding the reform of the 2002 Press Law, with special reference to the provisions covering defamation and prison sentences for press infractions.

The forum provided an opportunity for the National Press Syndicate to win the endorsement of the Ministry of Communication and the Federation of Newspaper Publishers for its collective-bargaining convention, which defines obligations for publishers vis-à-vis their staff and sets certain rights for journalists such as a minimum salary, holidays, health insurance, and further training.

Moroccan media-sector development in 2005 was highlighted by the promulgation of a new law liberalising broadcasting. This law turned state broadcasting into a public service and allowed the licensing of new private radio and television stations. The Higher Broadcasting Authority (HACA), (*la Haute Authorité de la Communication Audiovisuelle*), set up by a royal decree in 2002, launched a call for tenders to obtain private broadcasting licenses. HACA worked on the transition of the state television station into a public-service broadcaster and intervened in several conflicts between broadcasters and political parties, associations, and private companies. HACA is now the authority with the legal power to license new private radio and television stations. The organization's tender for those seeking new licenses received dozens of bids for radio stations and a few for television. The broadcasting sector in 2005 was made up of two public broadcasters, the *Societé Nationale de Radio Television* (SNRT) and 2M-spread. SNRT is composed of a national terrestrial channel, TVM, and three satellite TV stations: the educational channel Al-Rabi'a (the Fourth), Al-Maghribiyya (the Moroccan), a joint venture with 2M catering to Moroccans living abroad, and As-Sadissa (the Sixth), a religious television station. Arriyadia (Sports) and Aflam (films) and Medi -1 Sat private channels were also created in 2009 and there is one regional station in the city of Layoune. The public radio network is made up of one national and 14 regional stations. Medi 1, located in Tangiers, the US-funded Radio Sawa and fourteen others are privately owned. It was also decided to establish in 2009 a television station exclusively for Amazigh (Berber language).

Eleven authorisations were granted on 10 May 2006 to establish private radio and television networks. A new TV channel " Médi I Sat" , two radio stations in Marrakech and Agadir; four regional radio stations covering Casablanca, Fez, Meknes and Marrakech; a regional radio spécialising in music for Casablanca and Marrakech; a regional radio station covering the North of the country and the Eastern region of the Rif; a regional radio station specialising in economic and financial affairs covering Rabat and Casablanca and a regional radio station specialising in economic affairs covering the cities of Rabat, Casablanca, Fez and Meknes.

Licences for ten more independent radio stations were granted in 2009 and others regarding television channels are pending.

HACA is run by a nine-member council, five of whom are appointed by the King, including the president. The prime minister appoints two, and the last two are named by the presidents of the two chambers of parliament. HACA publishes on its website the required documents and the conditions that candidates must meet in order for their projects to be considered. One important aspect of the law is the exclusion of associations and political parties from ownership. The public broadcast sector does not receive any legal preferential treatment, and the new broadcasting law guarantees, in theory, its editorial independence. Article 4 of the broadcasting law provides that, "subject to the preservation of the pluralist character of expression, the broadcasting companies freely conceive their programmes and assume responsibility for them." The law obliges public broadcasters to be open to all political and ideological voices in the country. Article 8 of the broadcasting law requires public broadcasters to offer objective and pluralistic information without any bias toward a political party, interest group, or association. It also requires these broadcasters to cover the King's activities, debates in parliament, and other government activities as priorities. Article 3 urges public broadcasters to produce programmes that respect religious values, public order and good behaviour as well as the preservation of national security.

The new broadcasting law that liberalised the airwaves allows for the creation of more private television and radio stations and it is expected that the number will grow.

In addition, international radio stations and multi-lingual satellite television channels are widely used by the majority of Moroccan homes and play an increasingly important role in influencing people's every day's life. So much so that people do not feel the need to buy the print media when they are exposed on a daily basis to virtually hundreds of international channels free of charge.

Government officials have begun to discuss amendments to the country's press law that call for the establishment of a national press council with the power to withhold advertising and ban journalists for purported ethics violations. It is hoped that these amendments will be adopted by parliament by the end of 2009. Morocco's print press has made important strides since the 1990s and even now ranks among the most critical and vibrant in the Arab world and the African continent. With 18 dailies and scores of periodicals in French and Arabic, private publications represent pro-government, opposition, and independent views.

The Moroccan press faces a double challenge when it seeks to operate according to contemporary western press freedom standards.

Political traditions inherited from the French system of government and media code of ethics, coupled with the traditional monarchical system, have created a legal framework that allows the government to choose how to interpret certain legal conditions that enable it to restrict the flow of information. Government officials and many Moroccan journalists have played down recent restrictions on the press, choosing to regard them as isolated incidents and preferable to the not-so-distant days of political repression and censorship.

The monarchy in Morocco remains a sacred institution and plays the role of a prominent arbitrator. Thus, it remains an important actor as well as a key factor in the reform process. The current monarchy's political reform policies are presented as a continuation of what has already been achieved; respectively, Mohammed V's steps to independence followed by Hassan II's social reforms. King Mohammed VI and his ministers find themselves in the awkward position of moving Morocco into the twenty-first century, of being politically pro-western while exemplifying the values of a moderate Islamic nation and consolidating the country's traditions and cultural heritage. They are also confronted with an Islamic fundamentalism that has become increasingly hardened and radicalised and poses a looming threat to the stability and security of the kingdom.

Although the present Press Code is under review and is not perfect, it nonetheless contains a number of positive beneficial elements, such as the insistence on criminalising racial incitement, hatred and violence that is based on sex, colour, ethnic origin and religion. The growing threat of terrorism, ever since the Casablanca bombings of May 2003, has led the authorities, especially the security forces, to become increasingly anxious to ensure the security of the country and its people. Violent extremism coupled with a growing Islamist movement has led both the authorities and many Moroccans to be more concerned with security considerations than civil liberties.

CASABLANCA - *Morocco's economic capital*

CHAPTER ELEVEN: ECONOMIC OVERVIEW

Economy

GDP (2008 est.):	$88.3 billion
GDP growth rate (2008 est.):	5.8%
Per capita GDP (PPP, 2008 est.):	$4,309
Natural resources:	Phosphates, fish, manganese, lead, silver, and copper.
Agriculture:	Products barley, citrus fruits, vegetables, olives, livestock, and fishing.
Industry:	Phosphate mining, manufacturing and handicrafts, construction and public works, energy.
Sector information as % GDP:	Agriculture 12.4%, industry 29%, services 58.5% (2007)
Monetary unit:	Moroccan dirham
Trade: *Exports* (2008 est.) Major partners (2007):	$20.6 billion f.o.b.; France 22.5%, Spain 17.6%, India 6.6%, Italy 4.2%, U.K. 3.6%.
Imports (2008 est.) Major partners:	$42.34 billion c.a.f. France 15.6%, Spain 10.1%, Saudi Arabia 6.8%, Italy 6.5%, China 5.7%, Russia 5.1%.
Budget (2009):	Revenues: $28.64 billion; expenditures: $30.21 billion. Debt, external: (2008 project): $18.8 billion

(source US Department of State)

The Moroccan economy has considerable potential for expansion: it has a sound agricultural base, though this needs modernisation, reasonable resources and a degree of diversity. Divisions exist between those who favour an open market economy and those who believe in substantial state or central controls and given the world recession, which has laid bare some of the flaws in the unregulated market approach, the concept of a completely open market should now be tempered with caution. There exists a "philosophical" approach among the educated that they should seek jobs in government or administration rather than in business. It is an attitude that needs to be overcome if Morocco is to realise its industrial and business potential. The country's geographical position as the meeting point of Africa and southern Europe and its easy communications between Tangier and Algeciras offer a ready access to the EU, which is Morocco's biggest market. The leading economic sectors are tourism, textiles and agriculture. Recent oil discoveries should be sufficient to meet the country's domestic needs for some 35 years. Fisheries and hydroelectric power are also of growing importance to the economy as a whole. The worldwide recession had not affected the country in mid-2009 but as EU countries cut back production in the face of lower demand this is bound to affect Morocco so that the expectation of growth in the economy will be tempered by the impact of world recession. EU expansion into Morocco will revert to slow motion as the rich economies rein in the level of their overseas investments. Thus, the plans by Renault and Nissan to open car manufacturing plants near the new free port of Tanger-Med to produce up to 400,000 vehicles a year by 2010 are likely to be scaled back in the short term.

The government is working to boost its tax revenues by evening out the tax base. It has introduced measures to increase consumption and economic growth in the private sector: as from January 2008 the business tax was lowered from 36 per cent to 30 per cent while the government promised to reduce VAT from 20 per cent to 18 per cent by 2012. Taxes for small and medium enterprises are to be lowered to 25 per cent and micro-enterprises will only be taxed at the rate of 2.5 per cent. However, these tax measures introduced by Prime Minister Abbas El Fassi, following his appointment after the 2007 elections, were not universally welcomed and 93 representatives in the Legislature voted against them on 30 October 2007. The government has devised what it calls the "Moroccan offer" strategy that aims to sharpen the country's competitive edge in the offshore sector by providing world-class infrastructure and training, and by offering a set of unique incentives. Morocco is beginning to be seen as a target country for investors from Europe and the Gulf and must continue to push through reforms that will create attractive investment opportunities.

New development projects are home generated; once underway, if they appear suitably viable, they will attract outside interest and investment. France is Morocco's leading trading partner and also the largest source of foreign direct investment. Economic relations with both France and Spain may be assisted by the past colonial relationship but neither country has a special position in the economy. Only Morocco, outside the EU, has a special associate status with it. The initiative of President Sarkozy of France to create a Mediterranean Union was warmly welcomed by Morocco as a proposition though as yet it has made little progress.

An influx of transnational corporations has transformed the telecommunications sector as well as leading to huge growth in the use of mobile phones while computer use is also steadily rising. So far Morocco has not benefited greatly from the boom in global outsourcing but the government hopes this will change as interest from the wealthy Gulf Cooperation Council (GCC) countries is growing. With political stability, a business friendly government, a good telecommunications and ICT environment and plenty of well-trained multilingual graduates, as well as geographical and cultural proximity to Europe, Morocco is well placed to obtain a significant share of the offshore market, and dedicated zones will be located in Casablanca and Rabat and subsequently in Fez. The target of the government's off shoring programme is to create some 100,000 direct jobs and contribute around Dh15 billion ($1.7bn) to GDP by 2015. So far, Morocco has attracted roughly half the French-speaking call centres that have gone offshore as well as a number of Spanish ones. The country has about 200 call centres, including 30 of significant size. They employ 18,000 people. According to Bachir Rachidi, Chairman of the Moroccan Federation of Information Technologies, Telecommunications and Off shoring, "Morocco is increasingly positioning itself as a key telecommunication partner for companies across the region, providing both a strong Arabic-speaking outsourcing destination, as well as sustaining major growth and investment opportunities." Outsourcing is assisted by Morocco's economic liberalisation and the country's willingness to embrace new global networks. During 2007, there was a big jump in the activity of call centres operating in Morocco and receipts increased by 35.7 per cent to $207 million. As of 2009, the IT industry was growing at the rate of 9.6 per cent a year.

There are more than three million Moroccans living outside the country and their remittances to families and friends add between $2bn and $3bn a year to the national GDP. Such income is of especial importance because it goes directly to individuals who can spend it at once on items of their choice in the market place, on education for their children or on establishing small businesses. As in other countries with substantial overseas populations sending money back home, its impact is far more significant than aid since it boosts the incomes of individuals and through them has a knock-on effect upon local markets. Spreading development and making sure that it has the widest impact is far from easy. One way of doing this is the establishment by the government of 16 Regional Investment Centres located in major cities throughout Morocco with access to key government ministries through the E-Government Cyber Network with the result that Morocco has now become one of the quickest places to set up business in the whole Middle East and North Africa (MENA) region.

No section of the economy is closed to foreign investment and all sectors are open to private initiative, both national and foreign. Morocco now has free trade agreements (FTAs) with the EU, the US, Turkey, the GCC countries and certain countries in Sub-Saharan Africa. However, an FTA does not necessarily make a significant impact on the economy. The FTA between the United States and Morocco, for example, is primarily a political gesture and will work to the advantage of the bigger power. US-Moroccan relations are good and the FTA is a measure of US-Moroccan friendship as much as anything else. So far it has not led to a great deal of trade. China, whose representatives these days appear throughout Africa, sees Morocco as a possible jumping off point for trade and investment in Sub-Saharan Africa and also, perhaps, for movement into the EU market. The most important trade partner and source of investment is the European Union and within it the two leading partners are France and then Spain though Britain has become an increasingly important source of tourists.

An IMF mission visited Rabat on 19-30 May 2008 to conduct Article

IV discussions. In its conclusions the IMF said Morocco was reaping the benefits from its reform efforts, in particular the implementation of sound economic and financial policies. Its achievements put Morocco in a relatively favourable position to absorb shocks arising from the developing world recession and recent economic results demonstrated the resilience of the Moroccan economy. Non-agricultural GDP had grown by an average of 5.5 per cent since 2004. Agriculture, however, had been adversely affected by climate changes and there had been a sharp fall in cereal production in 2007. Morocco's external position remained sound but while the level of exports had remained steady imports had grown faster due both to increases in volumes and also to sharp increases in the prices of food and oil. However, the outlook was less encouraging. The market deterioration in the international environment of 2008 presented new challenges. Slower growth, especially in the EU, which is Morocco's major market, would lead to a cutback in Moroccan exports to it. On the plus side, the strengthening of Morocco's fiscal position in recent years and a lower public debt burden had increased investors' perception of Moroccan credit worthiness. The IMF welcomed the government's intention to gradually unwind the current system of universal subsidies by targeting them to the poor. However, the IMF noted that any radical change to the system of subsidies would be difficult to implement although a reduction of subsidies for products mainly consumed by better off households could be implemented quickly. In its conclusion, the IMF pointed out that strong and sustained economic growth would require further reforms to improve the productivity of the economy, which has grown less rapidly than in the most dynamic emerging markets. Further, continued sectoral reforms, especially in agriculture, energy and domestic trade as well as education reform and strengthening of infrastructure and social services, would have a key role to play in boosting investment, production and employment as well as improving incomes.

Morocco is in no way aid dependent, which is a huge plus for any emerging market since it relieves the economy of further aid-related debts and eliminates the donor pressures that always accompany aid packages to adopt the economic policies that they prescribe. However, the economy faces a number of challenges. First, agriculture depends upon rainfall and this may vary sharply from year to year. Second, the education system is as yet a long way from turning out the skills needed to expand the economy. Third, and perhaps most damaging to swift development, not enough is invested in the population: development thrives on a rising standard of living and, in turn, the more prosperous people are the more they contribute to further development. Fourth, energy costs are very high. Each year some 460,000 rural migrants arrive in the cities to swell the poor ghettos. Meanwhile, the economic reforms of the last few years have not had the impact that was expected while unemployment runs at 10-11 per cent of the work force and two thirds of the population are in their twenties or younger. However, there is full employment in agriculture. The government is constantly seeking ways to create more jobs for the unemployed. One aspect of education that needs greater emphasis is for the creation of business schools re-orient and then train people to take up careers in business. Unemployment, illiteracy and education are at the top of the list of national problems. One political-economic question that stubbornly remains unresolved is that of the Maghreb Union. It has been estimated that a resolution of their differences between Morocco and Algeria, so that the Maghreb Union could begin to function as intended, would add one and a half per cent to Morocco's GDP. That consummation, however, must await a political resolution of Algerian-Moroccan differences.

CHAPTER TWELVE: TRADE, INDUSTRY AND AGRICULTURE

In mid-June 2008, as the world began to react to the recession, Morocco revised its projected annual rate of growth from 6.8 per cent to 6.2 per cent, still a very healthy outlook for a country whose economy is so closely tied to that of Europe. During the first half of the year tourism had increased by 11 per cent over the same period for 2007. Government planners expected to see an economic growth rate of 6 per cent for 2009. Industry and agriculture are a significant contributor to the country's GDP, ranging between 25 per cent and 35 per cent, depending upon agricultural performance and overall contribution. Foreign direct investment (FDI) is crucial to industrial development and investors tend to target the staple fertiliser and phosphates divisions first. Apart from agriculture, industry's share of GDP is 16 per cent. The present phase of industrial development began with the accession of King Mohammed VI in 1999 and the country has witnessed considerable industrial advances since that date.

The construction sector's requirements and the expansion of the cement industry are good indicators of the state of the economy. In July 2008, for example, Ciment du Maroc signed a $274m loan agreement with a consortium of five banks to fund the construction of a new factory near Agadir, a project that will cost $480m. Ciment du Maroc, the local subsidiary of Bergamo-based Italcement, which is the world's fifth largest cement producer, aimed to start production in March 2009; the plant will have a capacity of 2.2 million tonnes of cement and 1.6m tonnes of clinker a year. This new Agadir plant is designed to meet the growing demand for cement by Morocco's construction industry and rival the challenge of its two main competitors, France's Lafarge Ciments and Holcim of Switzerland, which are also investing heavily in the country and expanding their production. In 2007, Ciment du Maroc saw its profits increase by 17 per cent to $83.7m, so that it was able to secure the loan from the five banks despite a general tightening of credit. From 2000 to 2008 the cement market grew by an average of 8 per cent a year. This rate of growth reflected that of the real estate and construction markets.

Meanwhile, approximately $1.3 billion was being invested in the rural road network, while the motorway system was being overhauled. The government has pledged to build 150,000 new low-cost housing units a year and to allocate a total investment of $4.4 billion to the tourism sector by 2010. Whether the government will be able to meet its ambitious target of 150,000 housing units a year, however, will depend upon the prices of raw materials. The programme remains a government priority. Major projects such as the Rabat tramway or the Tanger-Med port project have been put out to tender and are in the process of being implemented.

Tangier-Med Port

In January 2009 King Mohammed VI launched the construction of the Tanger-Med industrial park. At the site of the port project the industrial park will boost output and take advantage of Tangier's proximity to Europe. Thus, at a time when recession means European economies are contracting, Morocco has an opportunity to offer high quality goods at a lower cost. Morocco intends to ride out the recession by building infrastructure to support renewed trade levels in the future. It will also rely upon consistent revenue earners such as phosphates and its derivatives. The Tanger-Med container port should be fully completed by 2012, when it will be among Africa's largest ports with a container handling capacity of 8.5m twenty-foot equivalent units (TEUs). Lying a mere 14 kilometres from the Spanish coast the port should greatly increase Morocco's profile as an industrial destination and serve as a logistics centre for the whole Mediterranean region. The purchase of 3,000 hectares of public land by the Tangier Mediterranean Special Agency (TMSA) will bolster the free trade zones that have sprung up near the port facility. Another agreement covers the development of a 5,000 hectare offshore zone near Tetouan. These zones were established in 2002. As of 2009, the Tangier Free Zone is home to 400 businesses and 40,000 jobs. The Melloussa Free Zone is to host the Renault-Nissan alliance to create an automobile industrial complex by 2010. Meanwhile, this zone is attracting private investment worth $1.3bn and generating 36,000 jobs. The new parks aim to attract a number of industries such as auto-parts, textiles, electronics and food production which fit in with government export plans. Under the 2006 Emergence Plan the government aims for a 16 per cent GDP growth over 10 years and the creation of 440,000 direct and indirect jobs.

Some 200 container ships a day pass through the Straits of Gibraltar. Such a concentration of traffic makes the coastal area between Tangier and Ceuta ideal for trans-shipping cargo, and unloading or picking up containers heading to or from ports that the individual vessel does not serve directly. For many years only Algeciras served such vessels. Its facility to serve containers was established in 1986 and was operated by APM Terminals, part of Denmark's AP Moller-Maersk Group, to become one of the world's most important centres, both for transfers between deep sea, mainline services and between these and smaller feeder ships heading for different destinations. The Algeciras markets include the ports of North and West Africa as well as destinations in the Americas and Asia. This Algeciras monopoly was broken in September 2007 when ships began to use the port of Tangier, where APM Terminals and a local partner have constructed the Straits' second big container terminal. A second terminal at Tangier is to be run by another consortium. These Tangier terminals will obtain a growing share of container traffic, partly because Algeciras has been so successful that it has reached its 3.6 million capacity of 20 foot equivalent units (TEUs). Tangier is attractive because there is no more room for expansion at Algeciras and because it also offers lower wage and land costs than its counterpart 10 miles to the north. Tangier is investigating how far it can branch out beyond the highly competitive trans-shipment market in order to boost the Moroccan economy. The attractions for Tangier are several. A ports analyst from the London-based Drewry Shipping Consultants has described the opportunities arising from mainline services using Tangier as boosting the economy because they will increase the connectivity of Morocco as a country. Both import and export cargos can move through Tangier where a free zone is being established next to the port. Tangier will soon have the capacity to compete with congested Algeciras. While Algeciras has the advantage of size, Tangier will have the advantage of lower costs. Although still under development, Tangier was expected to handle 500,000 TEUs in 2008 and reach its full capacity of 1.5 million TEUs during 2009. Although the Danish Maersk line has dominated container trans-shipment in the region, Tangier's second terminal is owned by a consortium of Eurogate (a German terminal operator) with Mediterranean Shipping Company, the world number two container carrier, and CMACGM, the number three. Rapid progress in port construction means that these two lines' vessels should regularly be heading out of the Gibraltar Strait transhipping containers as from the end of 2008.

Once complete, the Tanger-Med industrial park will help meet these goals and the hope is that the new site will create 300,000 positions within 20 rather than 10 years. The Tanger-Med port is already larger than that of Casablanca and by 2010 it should be the largest container port on the Mediterranean.

As the economy grows so also does the use of Morocco's roads. Legislation to regulate the use of the country's roads was introduced in February 2008 and finally approved by the Assembly of Representatives on 19 January 2009. It represented part of a broader plan for the transport sector. The plan was allocated a budget of Dh1bn (Euro90m). Traffic accidents cost the country Euro948m a year and are the leading cause of deaths in Morocco, causing 4,230 deaths in 2008 so that new regulations were urgently needed. Enforcement of such regulations is always a problem. The new law aims to reduce corruption and improve road network safety. Increased penalties cover speeding, drunk driving, running through red lights and using mobile phones while driving. Fines will go as high asDh900 (Euro81) while the accumulation of 24 penalty points will mean the motorist loses his licence. There are also plans to make every Moroccan's driving record available on a microchip attached to the licence, one of the uses of new technology to aid the police in tracking offenders. The passage of this traffic law coincided with a major initiative to upgrade the country's roads. This programme of road expansion was launched in 2008 by *Autoroutes du Maroc* (ADM) (the national road authority). The programme will include the construction of 1800kms of motorways by 2015 at a cost of Dh36bn (euro3.25bn). These will include four major projects: a ringroad round Rabat, already begun in 2009; a 172kms road linking Berrechid to Beni-Mellal, which will pass through Ben Ahmed, Khouribga, Oued Zem, Bejaad, and Kasbah Tadla; the expansion of the Rabat-Casablanca motorway; and a 140kms motorway connecting El Jadida to Safi. These motorway projects will assist the development of technologies in Morocco's construction companies to bring them up to international standards. Road investment will have a knock-on effect upon other sectors of the economy and will boost tourism, agriculture and industry.

Volatile oil prices in 2008 hit Morocco hard; it has some modest oil resources and more could be discovered but at present has to import 96 per cent of its energy requirements. In 2008 the oil imports bill rose sharply to $1.1bn in the first quarter, which was 69 per cent up on the comparable period for 2007. As a consequence of this oil shock, Morocco began to look at the development of alternative energy sources that included wind, solar and nuclear power. The government aims to have a tenth of the national energy balance and 20 per cent of national electricity production come from renewable resources by 2012. This is an ambitious goal since the current level is only one per cent. However, Morocco has a large and steady wind flow off the Atlantic and consistent sunlight so the potential for a major increase in renewable energy certainly exists. The Abu Dhabi National Energy Company, known as Taqa, has bought into Morocco's main wind power firm, Compagnie Eolienne du Detroit (CED). In June 2008, Taqa (75 per cent owned by Abu Dhabi Water and Electricity Authority) signed a memorandum of understanding with the French renewable energy firm Theolia for the development of wind power stations in Morocco. As part of the deal, Taqa took a 50 per cent stake in Compagnie Eolienne du Detroit (CED), which is Theolia's majority-owned Moroccan subsidiary. Theolia and Taqa plan to jointly bid for the tender to construct and operate a 300MW wind power farm near the coastal town of Tarfaya. These and other moves indicate how Morocco is coming to be seen as a worthwhile country in which to invest in major projects.

The country has a substantial infrastructure capable of supporting an active oil and gas industry. At present upstream potential is being developed. There is a range of hydrocarbon occurrences in Morocco but much exploration has still to be done. In Morocco, which is a distinct advantage, exploration can be carried on all the year round. There is a well-developed downstream industry, with refineries situated at Sidi Kacem and Mohammedia, which between them have a 7 million tonne handling capacity but at present only deliver 4 million tonnes. Known power reserves are: 60,000 tonnes of oil and 1,020 million cubic metres of natural gas (condensate) as well as oil shale deposits. Current exploration is widely dispersed, much of it offshore. The most important oil and gas fields in production are found in the Essaouira Basin on the coast, which produces both oil and natural gas, and the Gharb Basin in the north of the country producing natural gas. However, since domestic energy resources are far from sufficient to meet local demand, some 90 per cent of energy needs are met by imports, which include 6 million tonnes of crude oil.

In general the banking system appears to be sound and resistant to shocks. However, the IMF team which visited Morocco in May 2008 stressed the need for increasing openness of the economy and the need for the authorities, central bank and other supervisory bodies, financial sector, and economic operations to work for a more open economic and financial system and for the system as a whole to increase its capacity to manage risks. The IMF also stressed the need to develop insurance and capital markets. According to a report of the central bank in September 2008, the financial sector was weathering the global storm and the country was on track in its plans to float the currency. Bank Al Maghrib (Central bank) said that Morocco's efforts to open capital accounts and move towards a more flexible exchange rate were continuing, despite the disruption to the financial sector caused by the global credit crunch. The Dirham (local currency) is pegged to a basket of currencies. At this time the Moroccan financial system appeared to be reasonably strong. Non-performing loans (NPLs) were running at 6.5 per cent as opposed to 19 per cent in 2004 while interest rates had dropped. Four strong sectors were tourism, fertilisers, construction and automotive industries that between them help to diversify the country's economic base. In addition, foreign direct investment (FDI) had soared and, according to the IMF, would reach a level of 3.8 per cent of GDP during 2008 as opposed to 1.5 per cent in 2004. This financial stability has helped the government facilitate money movements out of the country, a fundamental necessity if FDI is to be attracted on a regular basis. In March, the governor of Bank Al Maghrib, Abdellatif Jouahri, said that a free float of the Dirham could be brought forward from its scheduled date of 2010. On July 15, an official of the central bank confirmed that it wanted to liberalise the currency regime sooner than originally planned. Such liberalisation would give greater control over its monetary policy to Morocco and provide a clearer picture of the economy to would-be investors. Once a free float of the currency was in place exporters and importers would have to be ready to face currency fluctuations. There were other risks the banking system would have to face, for example, the banks should beware of increasing their exposure to risks by expanding their overseas operations too rapidly.

As a constant trading nation for centuries and with a geographical location at the meeting of the Mediterranean and the Atlantic, bridging Africa and Europe, Morocco has always adopted an outward looking nature providing a historical centre of distribution and supply that has made it the regional engine for trade and commerce. This characteristic is reflected in the country's orientation towards Europe especially the European Union. Some two-third of all foreign trade is currently conducted with the EU. To increase exports, the government rewarded exporters with tax breaks and incentives.

The trading links with the EU are of paramount importance to the Moroccan economy.

Morocco's political stability has made it possible for the country to enter into a number of trade agreements with other countries. These include the Agadir Agreement of 2004, the FTA with the United States in 2006 and, most prized, the October 2008 agreement with the EU, which then granted Morocco "advanced status". France, Morocco's largest trade and FDI partner acted as an advocate for Morocco during the negotiations with the EU; subsequently, France supplemented the accord with several bilateral accords in the fields of defence, infrastructure, development, transport and tourism. Phosphates and its derivatives do attract FDI and this segment of the economy accounts for 33.4 per cent of all exports. Morocco's expanding list of investors and trade partners helps to foster broader market access for its industrial exports. However, agreements once concluded do not immediately result in mutual benefits and it is likely that such benefits will remain elusive until the recession bottoms out and the world economy begins to recover.

There are a number of things that Morocco has to do if it is to attract investors. It must ensure that there are adequate facilities and introduce a regime of low taxes to encourage incomers. During the first eight months of 2007 investment and foreign loans stood at $2.75bn, an increase of 7.4 per cent over the same period in 2006. Morocco requires a steady flow of FDI into the country if it is to achieve its development targets and it has become increasingly skilled at attracting inward investment and loans. It has taken a number of steps to improve the investment climate and from 2006 onwards has attracted the highest volume of FDI on the African continent after South Africa. In November 2007, the Kuwaiti Fund for Arab Economic Development

(KFAED) provided a loan of $55 million to improve Morocco's roads, connecting the inhabitants of remote villages by 500kms of rural roads. KFAED, indeed, has developed a particular interest in Morocco and this loan of 2007 brought its investments in Morocco up to $1.2bn. A major proportion of the country's FDI comes from France first, and then the Gulf and the countries of North Africa and Asia, which are now playing a growing role in the industrial sector, particularly in fertiliser and phosphates production.

Phosphates

In May 2008, the Moroccan state-owned phosphate company, Office Cherifien des Phosphates (OCP) signed a $1bn deal with Libya Africa Investment Portfolio (LAIP) for the construction of three phosphate derivative plants. The factories will produce phosphoric acid, ammonium hydroxide and fertilisers. One factory is to be constructed in Libya, another in the phosphate rich Jorf Lasfar region southwest of Casablanca, while the fertiliser plant will be located in one of the two countries following further negotiations. Just before this LAIP deal was concluded, OCP signed a $600m agreement with Hanoi-based Petro Vietnam Fertiliser and Chemical Joint Stock Company for the building of a diammonium phosphate (DAP) fertiliser plant due to open in 2011 with an output between 660,000 and one million tonnes. (DAP is a soluble fertiliser produced from phosphate acid and ammonia.)

OCP is a major global player in the phosphate industry and hold 45% share of the worldwide trade in phosphates and phosphoric acid. Morocco maintains a global market share of about 32% in phosphate product exports with 120 customers in 59 countries.

Although phosphate production dropped 7.2% in 2008 to 25.8 million compared to 27.8 million in 2007, exports increased substantially. Export sales of phosphates at FOB prices nearly trebled from Dh6.047 billion ($800) in 2007 to Dh17. 701 billion ($2.2 billion) in 2008, derived product exports more than doubled from 16,206 billion ($ 2.02 billion) to 33,676 billion ($4.20 billion).

OCP is in a unique position with more than 50% of the proven worldwide phosphate deposits located in Morocco or 85.5 billion m3. 44% (37.3 billion M3(is located in in Oulad Abdoun zone around Khouribga, 36% (31.1 billion m3) at the Gantour field near Youssoufia and Benguerir and 15.9 billion m3 in the Meskala deposits near the Chichaoua region. The balance of 1.1 billion m3 is in deposists at Boucraa in the Sahara.

Khouribga is also home to the biggest open sky mine ans the largest phosphate chemical platform in the world.

OCP has been a driving force of the Moroccan economy and export sales represent 20% of Morocco's total export revenues. The group share in Morocco's exports in 2009 is expected to increase to 35% from 18.1% in 2007. The group's investment programme for the period from 2008-2012 is estimated at Dh37 billion ($ 4.62 billion). This investment will be directed at three main areas namely raising the annual extraction capacity from 27 million tones to 50 million; developing 4 phosphate processing plants with a capacity of 40 million; and the movement of processed phosphate from the port of Casablanca to that of Jorf Lasfar, south of El Jadida.

Morocco experienced robust growth in 2008 but the global financial crisis will slow this substantially during 2009. Even so, the IMF expects FDI to equal 3.8 per cent of GDP in 2008. Nonetheless, despite the recession, the general outlook for the economy remains positive with growth in 2008 running at 6.2 per cent. However, Morocco's major export markets are in Western Europe and these are experiencing increasing difficulties. Although Morocco is prepared to seek suitable FDI from anywhere, it comes principally from Europe. Its short distance from Europe, especially Spain, its general stability and climate make it an attractive destination for EU companies that wish to establish offshore businesses. In 2006 Ernest and Young, an advisory service, carried out an "Attractiveness of Morocco Survey." Although Morocco has been modifying its "low cost" image, investors still expect it to remain competitive as to labour costs, real estate, and corporate taxation. However, the survey found that Morocco was in a transition period in terms of image and had to learn to manage a new, challenging league of competitors. While investors experience growing satisfaction with respect to the local environment they are also becoming more demanding about such criteria as education, accessibility, social climate and security. The most attractive sector in which to invest (over a three year period of examination) was that of tourism and leisure activities. The next sector covered telecommunications, infrastructure and equipment while the weakest sector was that of high tech services (and a drop in telecommunications). Morocco was seen as leading the race for potential manufacturing implantations and services such as off -shoring and regional head offices, ranking it above Tunisia and Egypt in North Africa. As Morocco shifted its image from low cost to one of higher quality, so it was moving into a new competitive division. Consequently, it must face new competitors with a similar profile to itself from East Europe. Above all, Morocco wants to attract investors from Northern Europe while, at the same time, remaining highly attractive to Euro-Mediterranean investors. Investors think Morocco should continue to focus on human capital (that is, training, management practices, international culture, and links between business and universities.) It should also pay attention to the quality of its infrastructure. This "Attractiveness" survey was requested by Morocco's Investment Directorate. The survey also recorded an increased appreciation of the quality of the environment; personal and property safety, stability of the social environment and the level of skilled labour. Calculations as to future attractiveness for FDI will be affected (as elsewhere) by the eventual impact of the world recession that got underway in 2008. The rating of major cities for FDI attractiveness was as follows: Casablanca 63, Tangier 46, Marrakech 25, Rabat 24, Agadir 9 and Fez 8.

Crucial to Morocco's development ambitions is the central question of trained personnel: whether the educational system is producing enough trained people to supply the engineers and other skilled personnel that are the essential investment that an expanding industrial sector requires. As of 2009, 180,000 students with marketable skills are turned out of the educational system each year: 60,000 from the universities and 120,000 from technical colleges. Parallel with the need for trained personnel is the problem of unemployment, currently running at 10-11 per cent of the workforce. The government hopes that lower taxes will allow – or persuade – companies to take on more staff though such an assumption is hardly realistic for companies presented with a lower tax bill are unlikely to forego the benefits by increasing their wage bills. Following the elections of 2007, El Fassi's Istiqlal Party pledged to create 1.3 million new jobs by 2012 and reduce unemployment by 7 per cent. Whether this target can be achieved under present economic conditions remains to be seen.

Agriculture

Morocco, with its Mediterranean climate, is lucky in its agricultural potential. Its temperate climate and 85,000 square kilometres of arable land provide agricultural possibilities that few Arab or North African countries can match. The agricultural sector provides a solid basis upon which development can be built. A few statistics are in order. There are 9,895,000 hectares (24,451,000 acres) or 22.1 per cent of total land area that is arable. This breaks down as follows: cereal production 43 per cent, plantation crops (olives, almonds, citrus, grapes, dates) 7 per cent, pulses 3 per cent, forage 2 per cent, vegetables 2 per cent, industrial crops (sugar beet, sugar cane, cotton) 2 per cent, and oil seeds 2 per cent. The majority of the indigenous population in the rural areas carries out subsistence farming on less than five hectares (12 acres). Both climate and rainfall in the northwest of the country make it an attractive area for agricultural development. In the rainy northeast barley, wheat and other cereals can be raised without the need for irrigation though not sufficient in quantity to meet the country's needs and production will drop in years of poor rainfall. In a good year the country produces two-thirds of the grains (wheat, barley and maize) that it consumes. Otherwise, Morocco is broadly self-sufficient in food production though it has to import, on average, about 40 per cent of the cereals and flour required for local consumption from the United States. Other food imports include sugar, coffee and tea. All together, agriculture employs 40 per cent of the workforce. On the extensive plains of the Atlantic coast olives, citrus fruits and wine grapes are cultivated, mainly using water from artesian wells. Other agricultural products include oranges, tomatoes, potatoes, early vegetables, olives and olive oil and these high quality products are major exports to the EU. There is a good and expanding wine industry and it should not be too long before Morocco exports labelled wines to Europe and elsewhere. Development experiments on growing tea and tobacco are progressing. Morocco is developing its irrigation potential and is aiming to bring one million hectares (2.5m acres) of land under irrigation.

The agricultural sector enjoys complete tax exemption. However, critics of the tax regime suggest that rich farmers and agricultural companies obtain too much benefit from this tax system while small, poor farmers struggle with high costs and get little support from the state.

Livestock breeding (sheep and cattle) is widespread and Morocco meets its own meat requirements and is aiming to be self-sufficient in dairy products. A tenth of the land is covered by forests, which are commercially valuable; timber requirements are met by harvesting the high level forests in the Middle and High Atlas mountains. The country is also self-sufficient in charcoal from its eucalyptus plantations. Morocco's fishing grounds in the Canary Current are exceptionally rich in sardines, bonito and tuna but Morocco has yet to develop a more modern fishing fleet and processing facilities. Instead, in 1996 it entered into an agreement with the EU over fishing rights and in return for an annual fee allows EU fishing vessels (mainly from Spain) to fish in its waters. Agriculture is, and should be, the most vital economic sector and its importance was illustrated in the third quarter of 2007 when a 20.9 per cent drop in agricultural output caused the national GDP growth to fall by 7.6 per cent. However, 2009 is expected to yield a bumper year in cereals and this will help growth. The country's economy and general growth depends heavily upon agriculture, which employs 40 per cent of the active work force. Together with tourism and overseas remittances, agriculture underpins the economy.

There are long-term problems for agriculture, mainly related to water. Most of Morocco's crops are highly rain dependent and with unpredictable precipitation, which may become more volatile with global warming, and underdeveloped irrigation systems, agricultural output can never be certain. According to the World Bank, Morocco is now using 90 per cent of its available water reserves and by 2035 about 35 per cent of the population will have less than 500 cubic metres per capita of water a year compared with 700 cubic metres today. Although broadly self-sufficient in foodstuffs, food vulnerability must be a matter of constant concern. When the summer drought resulted in an overall yield 61 per cent lower than the previous five-year average, the government had to import over three million quintals of wheat to cover the shortfall at a cost of $407 million. This led to price hikes in basic foodstuffs during September and October 2007 that caused widespread social unrest. Thus, future water shortages and food dependence pose major challenges. The government, which came to power in 2007 made a commitment to reform the agricultural sector and pledged Dh25 million

($3.2m) for agricultural research. A major agricultural development was launched in that year by Olea Capital to develop the world's largest olive oil production scheme. The aim is to plant 10,000 acres of land with 20 million olive trees divided between 10 farms for an investment of $223million. Modern methods should lead to an annual production of 30,000 tonnes of olive oil at a time when the world market for olive oil is expanding, especially in the United States. Moreover, the scheme should revolutionise the existing olive oil sector, which has stagnated.

Morocco's fourth world agriculture fair, which was held at Meknes in 2009, attracted 700 exhibitors and more than 700,000 visitors. The fair was opened on 22 April under the patronage of King Mohammed VI. It featured scientific and technical conferences and cultural events and provided an opportunity for Morocco to present its partners with details of its Green Plan. The plan, launched in 2008, aims to promote the competitiveness of the farming sector so that it becomes the driving force of the economy over the coming 15 years. The fair displays Morocco's agricultural products and acts as a showcase to attract international operators. The country is stepping up its agricultural development which now absorbs 40 per cent of the labour force, employs 80 per cent of the rural population and accounts for 16 per cent of the national GDP.

A country, however, is not just a process of development. It is about politics, human rights, social welfare, equality, growth and much else besides and all these aspects must develop side by side. Optimism about the future must be tempered by a number of problems such as the countrywide 40 per cent rate of illiteracy or the high level of unemployment that requires a constant search for new job outlets to absorb some of these unemployed and the new numbers coming out of schools and universities every year. These two problems – illiteracy and unemployment – are of particular concern to the government.

Analysis of foreign capital by major country source and industry sector

Country	Share of total foreign capital	Share of total capital	FOREIGN CAPITAL BY SECTOR			
			Agro-food	IMME*	Chemicals	Tex-tiles**
	%	%	%	%	%	%
France	25.69	4.14	11.99	34.95	44.31	8.75
Spain	15.73	2.53	25.83	9.92	52.23	27.93
Gt. Britain	9.12	1.47	68.96	0.09	16.22	14.73
Switzerland	7.95	1.28	16.39	2.29	54.26	27.0
Italy	6.99	1.13	5.80	57.98	30.89	5.34
Sweden	6.87	1.11	0	0	100.00	0
USA	3.75	0.60	1.42	46.60	16.49	35.49
UAE	3.45	0.56	6.46	42.22	51.33	0
Germany	3.17	0.51	2.66	79.31	6.85	11.18
Saudi Arabia	3.14	0.51	31.83	0	68.17	0
Belgium	2.60	0.42	2.04	4.24	84.18	9.54
China	1.64	0.26	6.66	0.59	0	92.75
Netherlands	1.45	0.23	9.63	48.26	38.47	3.63
Syria	1.13	0.18	8.86	4.43	11.60	75.11
Luxembourg	1.09	0.18	0	97.90	1.32	0.78
Japan	1.02	0.16	0	100.00	0	0
All others	5.21	0.84	n/a	n/a	n/a	n/a
TOTAL	**100**	**16.11**	**15.10**	**24.81**	**43.99**	**16.09**

*Note: IMME includes metallurgy, mechanical, electrical and electronic industries
**Note: Textiles includes clothing and leather

Source: annual survey of industries in transformation (2007): Department of Commerce and Industry

Saidia beach, near Ougda

Saidia golf course

Oasis in the Moroccan desert

Berber village in the Atlas Mountains

CHAPTER THIRTEEN: TOURISM

Morocco possesses huge tourist assets: dramatic scenery, high mountains and forests, ancient cities like Fez and Marrakech, climate, sailing, swimming, fishing and beaches with coastlines on both the Atlantic and the Mediterranean, excellent top quality hotels, distinctive Moroccan food and fine wines and friendly people. King Mohammed VI has set ambitious targets for tourism and infrastructure development and is determined that the targets should be achieved. His Vision 2010 aims to boost tourist arrivals to 10 million by 2010, a target that requires the addition of the number of available beds by 160,000.

The "Open Skies" policy adopted by Morocco in 2006 should lead to an expansion of tourism since it enables low cost airlines such as Easyjet and Ryanair to enter the market and make Morocco more accessible to budget tourists. A major aspect of Vision 2010 is the Plan Azur (Blue plan) or "intelligent seaside tourism" as the Ministry of Tourism describes it. Plan Azur will lead to the creation of six new resorts, five on the Atlantic coast and one on the Mediterranean. Up to the present time tourism has been focused on Agadir, Marrakech and Casablanca but the Plan Azur will open up new stretches of the country to sun seekers and holidaymakers. Meanwhile, Morocco is encouraging the expansion of new budget and charter airline routes from Europe. During 2008 estate agents reported a particular rise in the number of British property buyers. Moroccan brokers Atlas Immobilier said that 70 per cent of their clients came from Britain. There is now a revival of interest in the plan for a tunnel to link Tangier with Spain (the idea has been considered since the early 1970s). The increase in the number of tourists visiting Spain has led to a rethink of the tunnel proposition and a tunnel with a railway would substantially increase the Moroccan-Spanish trade. At present EU countries account for 78 per cent of Morocco's export revenues and a rail link would be of great benefit to both sides. Europeans make up the bulk of tourist arrivals in Morocco with the majority coming from France. Budget airlines have had a marked impact on the number of new tourists visiting the country, especially from Britain.

Tourist arrivals in 2008 reached 7.8 millions representing a rise of 6% compared to 2007.
Tourist arrivals by country of origin in 2008 were as follows:

Country	Number of tourists
France	2.9 million
Spain	1.7 million
Belgium	418, 000
Germany	405, 000
United Kingdom	359, 000
Italy	289, 000

Overnight tourists by numbers in 2008 reached 13.063.592, a drop of 5 % compared to the previous year and they are as follows:

Country	Numbers
France	5,936,414
United Kingdom	1,074,673
Germany	959,079
Spain	816,985
Belgium	590,868
The Netherlands	570,730

In 2007 tourist numbers visiting Morocco reached a high of 7.4 million, which was well on the way to the 2010 target of 10 million. This was the highest tourist tally in four decades. On 29 January 2008, the tourism and crafts minister Mohamed Boussaid said: "Tourism has become the chief source of investments and job creation in the Kingdom, as well as a driving force for sustainable development, contributing 8 per cent of the country's gross domestic product." One aspect of tourist strategy is the promotion of new beach destinations with six seaside resorts already licensed by the tourist industry. These will increase capacity by 111,000 beds of which 70,000 will be located in hotels. This expansion should generate 200,000 jobs. Tourism, however, can also be a trap. It brings in quick revenue but too much concentration upon new hotels and other tourist facilities could detract from the more important long-term investment in industry. It may be destructive as well as profitable and any expansion should be carefully monitored.

There are plans to create a human resources and training contract programme to meet the sector's need for qualified staff. Morocco, with its economic, cultural and human assets is expected to become a top Mediterranean tourist destination by 2010. According to the British e-paper "The Daily Reckoning", Morocco "is considered a good-value family destination with plenty of historical and cultural heritage, near and convenient for European travellers, but maintaining its unique charm." Morocco would like to diversify away from reliance upon France for the bulk of its tourists and instead rely more on all Western Europe. The country is also becoming attractive for second-home buyers, in particular from Britain, Germany and Switzerland. One large-scale project underway is The Morocco Film City, €1.3bn ($1.7bn) development near Marrakech to house film production studios, theatres, condominions, hotels and conference centres.

Tourism is now a crucial sector of the economy. Morocco has signed a $409m agreement with France to begin operations during 2009 to bring an additional 10,000 beds "on line" by 2013. The sector hopes to attract an additional $4.4bn in investment by 2010 as part of its Vision 2010 development programme. Meanwhile, ongoing projects include the expansion of hotel capacity to 250,000 beds (from 133,000 in 2006) and the construction of six new resorts (Plan Azur) for the development of sustainable coastal tourism. These coastal resorts will be located at Larache, El Jadida, Agadir, Essaouria and Guelmim on the

Atlantic coast and Saidia on the Mediterranean. The target is to increase tourist arrivals to 10 million by 2010. This ambitious target appears feasible though it may be set back somewhat by the recession and its impact upon European holidaymakers.

Morocco is also targeting domestic tourists under the Biladi Plan, whose purpose is to encourage domestic nationals to spend more. It is reducing hotel costs to encourage overnight stays and will build on the already high levels of expatriate spending. The Biladi Plan aims to encourage Moroccans to use the formal tourist sector, as opposed to the informal or grey sector, when taking their holidays in the country. Local tourists complain that foreign visitors often have access to lower hotel prices than Moroccans. This is because many foreign tourists travel in package tours and so benefit from block bookings and discounted rates. Many hotels are too expensive for the majority of Moroccans so that a black market in home-stays has developed with these costing as little as Dh100 ($14) a night (the average Moroccan income is $3000). According to the tourism and handicrafts minister, Mohamed Boussaid, "the bottom line is that the main constraint on the development of internal tourism is the lack of accessibility in the sector, which means we need to consider the spending power of our fellow citizens. The obstacle is therefore the cost of an overnight stay." The (domestic) target for 2010 is to increase the number of trips booked by domestic tourists in the formal sector from 1.1m in 2003 to 2m, and boost the number of overnight stays in registered hotels in Morocco to 6m. The strategy is to expand budget accommodation to bring prices down and to increase the number of conventional hotel beds specifically targeted at Moroccans by 11,000 by 2010, while 19,000 new campsites will be created in areas most popular with Moroccan tourists. A family should be able to stay in the new hotels for Dh200-Dh500 ($25-$62.5) per night, while pitching a tent at a campsite will cost Dh100-Dh150 ($12.5-$19). Finally, travel agencies will be encouraged to make bulk bookings so that local tourists can benefit from the same discounts as foreigners.

In order to increase its tourist take the government is creating a number of high-end or more affluent tourist resorts while also focusing upon the less affluent local tourist market. In the first five months of 2008, according to the National Tourism Observatory, 2.5 million tourists visited Morocco. This was an increase of 11 per cent on the same period in 2007. The bulk of foreign tourists either come from northwest Europe or from neighbouring Mediterranean countries.

Despite the global economic downturn and the financial crisis, the overnight stays recorded at classified tourist accommodation establishments in Morocco in April 2009 showed for the first time, since the beginning of this year, a +5% rise compared to the same month of the previous year.

The overnight stays increase recorded in April concerns most tourist destinations of the Kingdom (except for Rabat and Meknes), notably Marrakech (+6%), Agadir (+4%) and Fez (+30%) which hold nearly 94% of additional overnight stays.

The analysis per inbound destination shows that the major tourist markets contributing to this evolution at the level of overnight stays in April are: the Spanish market +89%, the German +15%, the Belgian+18%, and the Italian market +6%. However, the French and the English have witnessed a drop at the level of their overnight stays (-2% and -11% respectively).

Finally, the average room occupancy has indicated a slight decrease of 1 point to be set at 49% in April 2009 against 50% the preceding year.

Yearly evolution of the number of hotel beds

	2001	2002	2003	2004	2005	2006	2007	2008	Var. (%)
Marrakech	18876	20399	22109	28464	30648	35068	39550	44 394	12%
Agadir	21586	22716	25367	25605	25491	26660	27904	28 605	3%
Casablanca	7804	8219	8448	9334	9334	10850	12656	12 762	0%
Tangier	7295	6807	7017	7039	7165	7141	7371	7 431	1%
Fez	4035	5287	5880	5880	6268	6584	6802	7 224	6%
Ouarzazate	4730	5106	5021	5683	5915	6582	6716	7 006	4%
Rabat	4133	4367	4367	4364	4592	4592	4812	4 812	0%
Tetouan	4293	4384	4637	4743	4793	4047	3821	4 359	14%
Meknes	2137	2138	2162	2614	2730	2780	2936	3 139	7%
Essaouira	1286	1352	1352	1398	1971	2130	2618	3 322	27%
Others	20826	21322	23255	24124	25363	26796	28035	29 882	7%
Total	97001	102097	109615	119248	124270	133230	143221	152 936	7%

In order to allow tourism to play fully the role defined for it as a driving force of socio economic development of the country, a great deal of measures and actions have been adopted with an implementation planning, follow-up and assessement operations.

The 2010 strategy aims to reach the following objectives:

- To treble the accommodation capacity and to balance the product ;
- To train at least 70.000 professionals in different trades of hotel business and tourism,
- To plan the synergy between new beds and additional aircraft seats and treble the offer concerning air transport seats;
- To adopt a modern marketing strategy based on partnerships with tours operators, travel and tourism professionals, touristic regions and strengthening the promotional budget;
- To improve the welcoming structure, services and entertainment ;
- To restructure the organs of the State linked directly or indirectly to the tourism sector.

These are the main fundamentals in terms of quality and quantity for the "2010 vision" to achieve the sought-after objectives.

Apart from minor problems, the Moroccan tourist plan is unusual in that it is both pushing the high end of tourist development while also working to increase domestic (the low end) tourism, taking account as it does so of growing Moroccan incomes.

CHAPTER FOURTEEN: PROBLEMS AND PROSPECTS

Morocco has a per capita income of $2200 but like so many statistics this is misleading since a proportion of its people are either poor or live below the poverty line. It will take years of sustained effort to lift the poorest people, especially those living in the rural areas, out of poverty. This is not just a question of improved incomes and full employment but will also require major advances in education, housing and health. King Mohammed VI, who has now ruled the country for ten years, made plain on his accession that he was both a reformer and a moderniser. He is an active monarch, constantly moving about the country to see how developments are progressing. Morocco has a long proud history and its people reflect the interactions of Arabs, Berbers, Jews, and the strong European connections with Spain and France. The wealth of the country is derived first from its agriculture, and then its natural resources, especially phosphates (arguably it is lucky not to be an oil state), and a growing industrial sector. Its natural beauty of mountains and deserts and long sea coastlines make it an ideal holiday destination for Europe and the tourist industry is a major foreign exchange earner. In terms of its present developments – in agriculture, commerce and industry – there is no reason why Morocco should not become an important middle level economy, for the potential to do so certainly exists. The great majority of the people are Muslims while other religions are tolerated. The King and his government are determined to prevent the spread of fundamentalist extremism. In international affairs, Morocco is generally conservative, and has good relations with the United States while it pursues a policy of closer relations with Europe where its most important economic partners are to be found. The question of Western Sahara and its relations with Algeria pose complex problems that have yet to be resolved.

Modernisation and change rest in the hands of the King. The present dynasty has ruled Morocco since the 17th century and the monarchy is deeply respected. King Mohammed VI is both a secular ruler and the Commander of the Faithful, a role that makes him the final arbiter in Islamic affairs, and confers upon him religious authority that enhances his secular power. While increasing the role of the political parties, the

King still retains ultimate authority and he is the initiator of the reforms that have taken place during his reign. His principal reforms so far fall under three headings: restitution and compensation for former prisoners and exiles including the first truth commission in the Arab world; social reforms about family life and the position of women; and programmes such as the INDH to tackle both shanty town and rural poverty. The King is at heart conservative and cautious about changing the political system too quickly and subscribes to limited or "guided" democracy while ultimate power remains in his hands.

With ferment and extremism that ultimately ends in acts of terrorism in much of the Muslim world, Morocco walks a delicate tightrope between conservative Muslims and modernisers. The King and government parties are determined to prevent the advance of extremism in the Kingdom and have tightened the security forces for that purpose. The majority of Moroccans are moderate Muslims though the King fears that extreme sects may try to recruit the poorest people to their cause. The main population is a mixed Berber and Arab one and Morocco maintains ethnic and cultural stability and equality between the two groups and their Arab and Berber languages. The King has worked to reassure the Berbers of their full participation in the culture of Morocco and to this end has established a royal institute "to protect, revive and improve" Berber culture and integrate the Berber language into the educational system. A television station for Berber-speaking people will become operational during 2009. Although Tamazight, the Berber language, is not spoken or taught in schools, this is scheduled to change: the language is heard on radio and television. There is a dynamic movement to promote the Berber language and culture through newspapers, concerts and other cultural events and growing efforts are being made to encourage the wider use of the language and increase respect for Berber culture. Various pilot projects such as the construction of mosques, wells, roads and schools have been undertaken in the southern Souss region. These projects have been funded by Berbers from the region who are working abroad as part of the Moroccan diaspora and their remittances play a leading role in assisting the Berber cultural revival.

The Jewish people have been a presence in the Maghreb for 2000 years and both Jews and Muslims travelled north and prospered together in southern Europe for more than 700 years. In 1492, however, when the Jews refused to convert to Christianity, both they and the Muslims were expelled from Spain and sought refuge in Morocco where the Jews were accepted into the country's life. Moroccan leaders have always made the well being of the Jewish people a top priority. During World War II, when the Vichy government of occupied France announced that it had prepared 200,000 yellow stars for the Jews of Morocco to wear, King Mohammed V replied that he would need 50 more for him and his family. He refused to make any distinction between his citizens. King Mohammed VI has declared his religious, historical, and constitutional obligation to protect the rights, liberties, and sacred values of the Jews in Morocco. This commitment dramatically affected Morocco's reaction at the time of the terrorist bombs in Casablanca on 16 May 2003 when of the five terrorist bombs that were exploded, three were directed at Jewish targets. The King expressed his condolences at a Jewish centre, condemned the criminal acts of the terrorists, and reaffirmed his determination to protect Jews and all Moroccan society, awakening the national conscience and strengthening the bonds between its different people. Serge Berdugo, the president of Morocco's Jewish Community Council, has pointed out that the Jews in Morocco have a vibrant community, which includes 30 functioning synagogues and three school networks to which influential Muslim families send their children. Moroccan Jews serve as counsellors to the King, ministers, colonels, as members of parliament, judges and ambassadors. On Jewish holy days, Muslim authorities, as a sign of respect attend Jewish services. Although there are anti-Jewish extremists in Morocco as elsewhere, the government insists that Moroccan Judaism is an intrinsic and permanent part of the national culture.

Morocco is a multi-layered, hierarchical society with extremes of wealth and poverty that it will take a long time to even out. Poverty afflicts a significant proportion of the total population and major efforts will be required to raise the living standards of the poor to a more acceptable level. The King has made plain his determination to help his poorest subjects and the INDH programme represents a positive start despite the challenges ahead. People have to create their own prosperity; what governments can do is provide them with the tools – better health, education and literacy, and job opportunities. The King is also aware that if nothing is done to alleviate the dire poverty of some of his subjects, they may turn away from the government and become prey to extreme Islamist groups who would be happy to mobilise them for their own ends. Most Moroccans are Muslims and the tradition in the country is one of moderation and tolerance of non-believers and that is how the majority would like it to remain. But Islam is passing through a dangerous extremist phase, whose repercussions are to be encountered worldwide and at the present time threats of terrorism cannot be dismissed. In both 2003 and 2007 Morocco experienced terrorist outrages so that the threat is never far beneath the surface of everyday life. There are traditionalists who oppose the King's reforms in relation to women's rights and there are hard line extremists who will resort to violence if not stopped by the security services.

It is never easy to reform a conservative society and those who argue that the King has not gone far enough should understand the forces of conservatism both from Islamist fundamentalists and the entrenched power brokers from the previous era with whom the King must contend. The change to the Mudawana and the empowerment of women that the King has brought about represent a major challenge to conservatives, for what can be changed in law may not be changed in custom for years to come. Those who want further progress should accept with good grace what has been achieved so far – and then campaign for more. Once a process of reform has been initiated it cannot be reversed or halted and while considerable progress has been achieved over the ten years of Mohammed VI's reign, much remains to be done and there are huge problems to be overcome. These problems include the following: the reduction of poverty and unemployment; controlling Muslim radicals; reducing drastically the nationwide levels of illiteracy; encouraging greater political participation so as to encourage the emergence of a more open, democratic society; controlling the way the economy develops, with careful attention to transnational corporations and how they exercise their power.

Corruption is a universal problem and there are many temptations to it in a poor developing country. In his later years, King Hassan II encouraged civil society organisations to speak out, especially on the issue of corruption. In part this resulted from a World Bank report on Morocco that pinpointed corruption as a primary impediment to foreign investment and economic development. In 1999, the year in which he died, King Hassan II allowed the formation of a network of associations committed to the fight against corruption and though little seemed to change as far as corruption was concerned the rise of civil society organisations was to have a significant impact upon human rights. The corruption watchdog Transparency International judged Morocco quite harshly in 2008 when it placed it 79 out of 169 nations on its corruption perception index (Morocco had been placed 45 out of 100 in 1999). Another World Bank report in 2007 named corruption and clientilism as particular challenges for Morocco's economy to deal with. The Millennium Challenge Corporation, a US-backed development fund, granted Morocco a development package of about $700m in September 2007 to stimulate growth and good governance. This funding was directly linked to the recipient's progress in political rights and anti-corruption measures. King Mohammed VI has pushed the issue of fighting corruption. He allowed the establishment of a Moroccan chapter of Transparency International and encouraged newspapers to report matters of corruption. In October 2005, the King authorised the creation of an independent organisation to fight corruption. Despite these moves and measures, there is as yet little evidence that the anti-corruption drive has been successful.

The elimination of poverty for a large segment of the population represents the biggest long-term task facing the Moroccan government. Poverty can be tackled in a number of ways: by creating wealth that is available to all; by opening up poor areas to greater connection with the rest of the country; by providing education, combating illiteracy and training for specific tasks; and by giving the poor a sense of self-respect and engagement in the community as a whole.

The INDH programme represents a good start along these lines. In May 2005, the King announced a national initiative for human development (the INDH project) to fight poverty, marginalisation and exclusion. He then said that any exploitation of social misery for political purposes, especially to encourage extremism was unacceptable. In June 2006, the King visited some of the poorest parts of the country and announced a series of public works in an effort to pre-empt Islamist extremism. In May 2009, celebrations were held in a number of cities to mark four years of the INDH programme.

Education is a principal key to development. Morocco has a large pool of human resources available at a competitive cost, which could form part of a growing industrial-commercial work force. It is also producing as many as 60,000 university graduates a year. Yet much needs to be done to improve the educational system. About 47 per cent of adult Moroccans are illiterate of whom 60 per cent are women. The government is focusing upon primary education and also providing free adult literacy courses and upgrading the national vocational training institute. There is a post-colonial problem over the language of instruction in schools. Education was Arabised in the 1980s when French as the language of instruction was replaced by standard Arabic. Now students begin elementary school with standard Arabic although this is unfamiliar to many. Students switch to French for advanced studies. Many reforms under Mohammed VI have been concerned with education, especially in rural areas where schooling is seen as a key to eradicating poverty. A government survey published in 2007 showed that the national illiteracy rate among those aged 10 years and above fell from 43 per cent in 2004 to 38.5 per cent in 2006. If this level of reduction can be maintained, it will mark real progress. El Habib Nadir, head of the national campaign against illiteracy, hailed these "encouraging results" as a vindication of the government's strategy. He said that the information that had been accumulated would help his agency allocate resources to particular segments of the population where illiteracy rates were especially high. One crucial statistic illustrates the size of the illiteracy problem: 60 per cent of those working in the agricultural sector, which creates 40 per cent of Morocco's income for a population of over 32 millions, cannot read. Nadir said his office was working with the Ministry of Agriculture to give special attention to this group. High illiteracy among other groups had led to similar cooperation with the ministries of fisheries, Islamic affairs, justice, national development and youth. In 2007, approximately 670,000 Moroccans were taking part in various literacy programmes while more than two million people had participated in such programmes between 2002 and 2006. The government is working to increase the number of children enrolled in school although 15 per cent of children between nine and 14 remain outside the formal school system. The government announced in 2007 plans to promote civic values in the schools. These would be similar to existing programmes to improve awareness of human rights. The object would be to teach students the benefits and responsibilities of citizenship in the same way they learn history or mathematics. In May 2007, the King said the programme's target was "to raise citizens who are committed to the immutable religious and national values of their country, who respect its fundamental symbols and open cultural principles, who are deeply attached to their varied, yet cohesive identity, who are proud of who they are, and who have a deep awareness of their rights and obligations."

Providing better housing is an equally important aspect of the social revolution: decent housing aids respect. According to official statistics in 2006, 350,000 slum dwellings in shanty towns were to be eradicated and replaced at an estimated cost of euros2.8 billion while euros800m a year is required to eliminate the annual deficit in housing construction at the rate of 40,000 units a year, which is the average rate at which shanty town dwellings proliferate. The social costs of eliminating poverty – education, housing and health – are easy enough to quantify; the problem is finding adequate resources of money and trained personnel to implement the programmes. The INDH project is being funded in part with aid from the World Bank and Spain but the problems grow as fast as the remedies are applied. The statistic that 40,000 new housing units a year are matched by the annual proliferation of 40,000 new shantytown dwellings tells the story. However, the government is determined to fight the spread of shantytowns around the big cities throughout the country and this may eventually lead to tangible results.

The political parties forming the present government tread carefully in a controlled situation in which they have little real power. They are neither very potent nor impressive and need to organise grass roots support if they are to become more acceptable as representatives and therefore better trusted by the people. Fear of extreme politics has become a guiding principle in present day Morocco with the consequence that the parties have accepted office partly to ensure that more radical (Islamist) movements do not come to power and they have adopted what might be called the politics of restraint. King Mohammed VI has said Morocco is not ready for full western style democracy. The emphasis is upon a moderate society in a world where violence and extremes are too often the norm. International monitors said the 2007 elections were free and fair; however, it is important to ask how much power the politicians actually wield? There is no strong figure standing up to the regime in a critical way and asking relevant questions. The King has been described as the "guardian of the poor"; ultimately, he is also the guardian of the political system and as such is determined that it should be a moderate system though how long such a relationship is sustainable remains to be seen.

The priorities of Morocco's foreign policy are clearly identifiable in a descending order that puts relations with the EU at the top of the agenda and this includes relations with the two European countries with which Rabat has closest relations – France and Spain. Next in importance comes the United States, and here necessarily the relationship is one-sided. The US sees Morocco in strategic terms and the two countries work together on security issues. Otherwise, Morocco looks to the US for better terms of trade and as a possible source of FDI. Nonetheless, the relationship is long lasting and appears to work well. Relations with the Arab world, ironically perhaps, are more difficult to quantify. The long-standing face-off between Morocco and its neighbour Algeria is a tragedy for the two countries but also for the Maghreb region as a whole since a rapprochement between Algeria and Morocco would give a huge economic and political boost to the Maghreb Union. Relations with the rest of the Arab world are generally good – there is considerable Gulf investment coming into Morocco, especially from Kuwait, Qatar and the United Arab Emirates – though Morocco does differ from other Arab countries in its attitude towards its Jewish minority since in its turn this affects its relations with Israel. While relations with countries such as Mauritania and Senegal in Sub-Saharan Africa are satisfactory, its withdrawal from the Organisation of Africa Unity (OAU) over the Saharan issue in 1984, has meant that Algeria has been able to lobby for support in its stand over Polisario and Western Sahara without meeting counter-diplomacy from Morocco. Finally, there is the 2007 proposal by French President Nicolas Sarkozy for a Mediterranean Union which was warmly received by the King. This Union, formed in July 2008 in Paris, may prove a step closer to a free trade zone between countries of the North and South flank of the Mediterranean.

It is far from clear how long the world recession is going to last or what impact it will have upon small economies which, like Morocco, look to Europe as their principal market and source of FDI. Morocco will be affected to some degree by the recession yet GDP is expected to grow by 5.7 per cent in 2009. If this level of growth is sustained it will be a considerable achievement, given that Morocco's major export markets are in the EU. However, like the other countries of North Africa, Morocco must face the prospect of shrinking export markets, fewer tourist arrivals and less FDI. Nonetheless, officials insist that the local financial system is in good shape while admitting that an international slowdown will pose a threat to growth expectations and development targets, which will have to be scaled down. In October 2008 the Governor of the Central Bank, Abdellatif Jouahri, said: "There is no impact on our financial system. But the recession could affect tourism, exports and foreign investment. So far the impact is slight but we need to be cautious." Morocco aims to attract 10 million tourists a year by 2010 but a slowdown in the European market that leads individuals to retrench their expenditure may mean that this target is not reached. On the other hand, as Jouahri argues, the crisis may provide Morocco with opportunities such as increased demand in Europe for its cheaper agricultural workers. Remittances from Europe-based workers are a big support to the economy. At the same time, it is possible that low-skilled workers in Europe may be among the first to be laid off, depending on how long the recession lasts.

Free speech and an independent media are among the most important measures of an open society. Both human rights and thriving politics depend upon free speech as an instrument to forward their influence. As King Mohammed had declared in an interview in July 2001: "Of course I am for press freedom, but I would like that freedom to be responsible --- I personally appreciate the critical role that the press and Moroccan journalists play in public debate, but we need to be careful not to give in to the temptation of the imported model. The risk is seeing our own values alienated --- There are limits set by the law". The Moroccan government accepts all sorts of political criticism but tolerates no attack on the monarchy or Islam. Journalists and newspaper editors are considered professionals who must report the news, but they are also considered educated, patriotic citizens who should be mindful of their social responsibilities to the public. If newspapers in Morocco expect to remain in business, they must agree to exercise some form of restraint and to practice self-censorship. An annual government subsidy to Moroccan newspapers is a welcome financial boost but at the same time a useful means to prevent some of the Moroccan publications from operating with full autonomy and independence. By western standards, however, the very existence of such subsidies is difficult to reconcile with the establishment of an autonomous and free press. The country's most assertive political publications are those willing to scrutinise the activities of powerful personalities, track corruption, and tackle sensitive political issues. Article 4 of the broadcasting law provides that, "Subject to the preservation of the pluralist character of expression, the broadcasting companies freely conceive their programmes and assume responsibility for them." The law obliges the public broadcasters to open up to all political and ideological voices in the country. The Moroccan National Press Union points out that the number of newspaper readers has stagnated and does not exceed 300,000 in a nation of 33 million. This puts Morocco among the lowest Arab countries in terms of newspaper circulation per 1,000 inhabitants. According to UNESCO, there are 13 newspapers for each 100,000 people. High illiteracy rates keep circulation very low and give food for thought about the limit and the influence of the print media on public opinion. There are calls for amendments to the press law and the establishment of a national press council. Revisions, however, may leave intact vaguely worded prohibitions against disrespecting the monarchy, Islam, and defaming state institutions such as the judiciary.

The government has a stake in RTM and 2M, Morocco's main TV networks. However, there is an expansion of private TV and radio services taking place. Of six newspapers and two weeklies, one is government owned, a second is a semi-official daily, three are private dailies and one a business daily, and two are private weeklies. Of four television stations, one is state run, one is partly state-owned, a third aimed at Moroccans living abroad is operated by RTM and 2M and the fourth, Medi I Sat, is a satellite channel based in Tangiers, and privately owned by Moroccan and French concerns. Of radio stations, one is state run and operates national networks in Arabic and French, and regional services, while a second is privately owned by Moroccan and French interests and based in Tangiers.

It is not easy to summarise the state of a nation but as one highly placed "political" Moroccan said: "The future of Morocco should be reasonable if three conditions are met: these are, if political parties become stronger, if current reforms are pushed through, and if there is no development of political Islam". During the decade that King Mohammed VI has been on the throne a number of important reforms have been pushed through but it is one thing to enact a law and something quite different to see that it is obeyed and practiced. There was, and is, opposition to the changes in the family law that go a long way towards establishing equality for women and, more generally, opposition to any change that upsets the old order of things. At the present stage in Morocco's history, it is vital that the momentum for change is maintained. All initiatives come directly from the King or, if they do not, they will get nowhere without the King's approval. King Mohammed VI is in a uniquely powerful position. He has presided over a decade in which the economy has achieved steady growth and expansion while he has initiated a number of groundbreaking reforms. But as history teaches, the reformer must not stop. The list of problems to be addressed over the next decade is a long one and the King will need all his skill and courage to deal with them.

Rabat - *Administrative capital of Morocco*

Marrakech - *Main tourist destination*

APPENDIX

TREATY ESTABLISHING THE ARAB MAGHREB UNION

Non official translation

In the name of Allah, the Most Merciful, the Most Compassionate,

- His Majesty King Hassan II, King of the Kingdom of Morocco;
- His Excellency Zine El Abidine Ben Ali, President of the Republic of Tunisia;
- His Excellency Chadli Ben Jedid, President of the People's Democratic Republic of Algeria;
- His Excellency Leader of the First of September Revolution, Colonel Mouamar El Kadhafi, President of the Great Socialist People's Libyan Arab Jamahiriya;

Having faith in the close-knit bonds binding the peoples of the Arab Maghreb and founded on a common historical, religious and linguistic heritage;

Responding to the profound and firm aspirations of these peoples and their leaders alike to establish a Union that shall further reinforce the existing ties between them and enhance the possibility of committing the appropriate means to a greater integration;

Being aware of the effects that would result from such an integration, and which would allow the Arab Maghreb Union to acquire weight and significance in such a way that it would contribute effectively to the world balance, consolidate peaceful relations within the international community and promote international peace and security;

Given that the edification of the Arab Maghreb Union entails tangible realizations and the establishment of common regulations which would concretize an effective solidarity between its components and give a boost to their economic and social development;

Expressing their sincere determination to make the Arab Maghreb Union a means for achieving complete Arab unity and a springboard for a larger union, encompassing other Arab and African states;

HAVE AGREED ON THE FOLLOWING:

Article 1

By virtue of the present Treaty, a Union called the Arab Maghreb Union shall be established;

Article 2

The Union shall aim to:
- Reinforce the bonds of fraternity binding the Member States and their peoples;
- Realize progress and prosperity for the Member States and defend their rights;
- Contribute to the maintenance of peace based on justice and equity;
- Pursue a common policy in different domains;
- Work for the progressive realization of the free movement of persons, services, goods and capital;

Article 3

The aforementioned common policy shall aim at achieving the following objectives:
- On the international level: to achieve concord between the Member States and promote close diplomatic cooperation based on dialogue;
- On the defence level: to safeguard the independence of each of the Member States;
- On the economic level: to realize industrial, agricultural, commercial, and social development of Member States through the commitment of the necessary means, particularly the launching of common projects and the elaboration of global and sector-based programmes;
- On the cultural level: to establish cooperation aimed at promoting education at different levels, preserving the spiritual and moral values inspired by the magnanimous teachings of Islam, and safeguarding the Arab national identity through the capitalization on appropriate means such as the exchange of teachers and students, the creation of academic and cultural institutions, as well as the establishment of Maghreb institutes devoted to research;

Article 4

-The Union shall comprise a Presidential Council composed of the Heads of State. This Council shall be the Supreme body of the Union;

-The Heads of State shall hold the Presidency of the Council for a period of one year, which shall be rotated amongst all Member States;

Article 5
The Presidential Council shall hold its ordinary sessions once a year. However, the Council shall be able to hold extraordinary sessions if need be;

Article 6
Only the Presidential Council shall have the right to make decisions. The decisions shall be made unanimously;

Article 7
The Prime Ministers of the Member States, or those assuming their function, shall be able to hold meetings if need be;

Article 8
The Union shall comprise a Council of Foreign Affairs Ministers, which shall prepare the sessions of the Presidential Council and examine the questions submitted to it by the Follow-up Committee and the Specialized Ministerial Committees;

Article 9
Each Member State shall designate, among the members of its Government or its General People's Committee, a member who shall be in charge of the Union's Affairs. These members shall constitute a Follow-up Committee and submit the results of its work to the Council of Foreign Affairs Ministers;

Article 10
The Union shall comprise Specialized Ministerial Committees set up by the Presidential Council which shall define its attributions;

Article 11
The Union shall comprise a Permanent Secretariat General, which shall be set up by the Presidential Council. The Presidential Council shall fix the Head Office for the Secretariat General, define its attributions and designate the Secretary General;

Article 12

The Union shall comprise a Consultative Council composed of thirty representatives from each Member State, designated by the legislative bodies in the Member States or in conformity with the internal regulations in each Member State;

- The Consultative Council shall hold annual ordinary sessions. It shall also hold extraordinary sessions at the Presidential Council's request;

- The Consultative Council shall deliver its opinions on every draft decision submitted to it by the Presidential Council. It shall also be able to submit to the Presidential Council all the recommendations susceptible of reinforcing the Union's action and realizing its objectives;

- The Consultative Council shall elaborate its own statutes and submit it to the Presidential Council for approval;

Article 13

- The Union shall comprise a Judicial Authority composed of two judges from each Member State, designated for a period of six years. Half of the members shall be renewed every three years. This Authority shall elect its president from amongst its members for a period of one year;

- The aforementioned Authority shall, among other others, rule on disputes related to the interpretation and application of the Treaty and agreements concluded within the framework of the Union, submitted to it by the Presidential Council or one of the States parties to the dispute, and that in conformity with the provisions stipulated in the Authority's statutes. Its judgments shall be enforceable and final;

- The aforementioned Authority shall deliver advisory opinions on legal questions submitted by the Presidential Council;

- The aforementioned Authority shall prepare its own statutes and submit it for Presidential Council's approval. The statutes shall be an integral part of the present Treaty;

- The Presidential Council shall fix the Judicial Authority's Head Office and decide on its budget;

Article 14

Any aggression against any Member State shall be considered as an aggression against the other Member States;

Article 15

- Member States shall not allow on their respective territories any activity or organization which would threaten the security, territorial integrity or political system of any other Member State;
- Member States shall also agree to abstain from adhering to any pact, or military or political alliance, which would jeopardize the political independence or territorial integrity of any Member State;

Article 16

The Member States shall be free to conclude bilateral agreements, among themselves or with other States or groupings, as long as these agreements do not violate the provisions stipulated in the present Treaty;

Article 17

The other Arab or African states shall be able to adhere to the present Treaty on condition that all the Member States accept;

Article 18

The provisions of the present Treaty shall be amendable at the request of any Member State. The amendment shall come into effect following its ratification by all the Member States;

Article 19

- The present Treaty shall come into effect following its ratification by all the Member States, in conformity with the procedures followed in each state;
- The Member States shall take the necessary measures in this regard within a maximum deadline of six months starting from the signature of the present Treaty;

Done in Marrakech, on Friday 10 Rajab 1409 Anno Hegirae (corresponding to Feb, 17 1989):
- On behalf of the Kingdom of Morocco: Hassan II
- On behalf of the Republic of Tunisia: Zine El Abidine Ben Ali
- On behalf of the People's Democratic Republic of Algeria: Chadli Ben Djedid
- On behalf of the Great Socialist People's Libyan Arab Jamahiriya:

Mouammar Kadhafi
- On behalf of the Islamic Republic of Mauritania:
Mouaouya Ould Sidi Ahmed Taya

DECLARATION OF THE CREATION OF A FREE TRADE ZONE ENCOMPASSING THE MEDITERRANEAN ARAB COUNTRIES

Non official translation

Morocco, Jordan, Tunisia and Egypt have resolved to work for the establishment of an enlarged Free Trade Zone encompassing the Arab Mediterranean countries.

The four countries charged a group of experts to sustain the political framework and set up the mechanisms required for the creation of the aforementioned Zone.

On Tuesday 8 May 2001, at the Royal Palace in Agadir, His Majesty King Mohammed VI, accompanied by His Royal Highness Prince Moulay Rachid, presided the signing ceremony.

The text of the declaration was signed by:
- Mr. Mohammed Benaissa, Minister of Foreign Affairs and Cooperation on behalf of the Government of the Kingdom of Morocco.
- Mr. Abdelilah Alkhatib, Minister of Foreign Affairs on behalf of the Government of the Hashemite Kingdom of Jordan.
- Mr. Amr Moussa, Minister of Foreign Affairs on behalf of the Government of the Arab Republic of Egypt.
- Mr. Habib Ben Yahya, Minister of Foreign Affairs on behalf of the Government of the Republic of Tunisia.

Text of the Declaration
"At the initiative of His Majesty King Mohammed VI, and in application of the resolutions of the 13th Arab Summit held in Amman, the Hashemite Kingdom of Jordan, the Governments of the Kingdom of Morocco, the Hashemite Kingdom of Jordan, the Republic of Tunisia and the Arab Republic of Egypt,

Convinced of the importance of sustaining common Arab cooperation, and in order to establish and develop the Great Arab Free

Trade Zone and contribute to the efforts exerted with a view to creating a common Arab market,

Given the bilateral agreements binding these countries, and in connection with the partnership conventions concluded with the European Union,

Convinced of the necessity to establish a strong economic space with a view to achieving a global development susceptible of standing up to the challenges, the constraints and the requirements of globalization, in conformity with the Charter of the Arab League and with the principles stipulated in the conventions of the World Trade Organization,

In prospect of the 2010 events related to the creation of a Euro-Mediterranean Free Trade Zone,

Considering the significance of the action for the liberalization of economic exchanges and the importance of partnership among the Mediterranean Arab countries, through new methods adapted to modern economic orientations at the regional and international levels,

The following has been decided:

1- Work for the creation of an enlarged Free Trade Zone encompassing the Mediterranean Arab countries, open to other Arab countries.

2- Charge groups of experts, representing the four Member States, to sustain the political framework and set up the mechanisms required for the creation of the said Zone.

3- Hold periodical meetings of the groups of experts with a view to preparing the draft convention on the creation of the enlarged Free Trade Zone.

4- Set up a High Official Committee charged with assessing the reports of the groups of experts with a view to submit a global approach, as soon as possible, to the Foreign Affairs Ministers".

MEDITERRANEAN FORUM (FOROMED)

I. MEMBERS

Algeria, Egypt, France, Greece, Italy, Malta, Morocco, Portugal, Spain, Tunisia and Turkey.

II. BRIEF HISTORY

There have been many ideas and initiatives of establishing cooperation in the Mediterranean. However, due to the constraints posed by developments in the Middle East, the desired results have not materialized. That is why the Mediterranean Forum, also referred to as Foromed came into being. This "Like Minded" grouping was formed on the initiative of Egypt and France. Its first meeting was held in Alexandria on 3-4 July 1994 where the "Mediterranean Forum" was founded with the participation of Algeria, Egypt, France, Greece, Italy, Malta, Morocco, Portugal, Spain, Tunisia and Turkey.

At its outset, three working groups were created; namely the "Political Working Group", the "Economic and Social Working Group" and the "Cultural Working Group". During the Political Working Group meeting held in Tunis on 12-13 April 1996, it was decided that the Senior Officials Meetings ought to be merged with the Political Working Group and the Economic and Social Working Group ought to be merged with the Cultural Working Group and renamed the Economic Working Group.

During the Senior Officials Meeting held on 9 February 1998 in Madrid, it was agreed to that the flexible nature of the Forum ought to be guarded, while at the same time more emphasis ought to be given to the economic and cultural chapters. It was also agreed to that, whilst protecting the independance of the Forum, the Forum ought to assist the Barcelona Process.

The Second Ministerial Meeting was held in Saint-Maxime, France on 8-9 April 1995. During this meeting discussions focused on the future of the Forum and its objectives. Another issue which was deliberated upon during the meeting was the candidature of other states who were interested in joining the Forum. As a result of deliberations it was agreed to that there would be two prerequisites for becoming a member : The first was that the country needed to be Mediterranean (littoral) and the second was that there needed to be a consensus on the membership. It was decided that for the time being no new members would be admitted and that the Forum would continue under its present composition.

Again at this meeting, the priority areas of cooperation put forward by the Economic Working Group was adopted and in this regard it was agreed to that the economic and social disparity between the north and south of the Mediterranean ought to be diminished, and that the level of welfare developed whilst giving more importance to regional integration and the expansion of trade. There was also a general consensus on the fact that duplication with other fora ought to be avoided.

The Third Ministerial Meeting took place in Ravello-Italy on 9-10 May 1996, where it was reiterated that when the time was right, enlargement of the group would take place according to the criteria set forth (being Mediterranean and on the basis of consensus).

The Fourth Ministerial Meeting took place in Algiers-Algeria on 11-12 July 1997, where it was decided that the informal nature of the Forum ought to be protected and that the Forum members ought to concentrate their activities on developing ways on preventive diplomacy, continuous dialogue and understanding among each other.

The Fifth Ministreal Meeting took place in Palma De Mallorca on 20-21 April 1998, where the Ministers had an in-depth exchange of views on how to reinforce their action to respond to the challenges they must meet to enhance stability and security in the region.

The Sixth Ministerial Meeting took place in St-Julian's, Malta on 4-5 March 1999 where the Ministers deliberated mainly upon the Euro-Mediterranean Peace and Stability Charter, which was also the focus of the meeting which was held in Palma de Majorca-Spain in April 1998.

The Seventh Ministerial Meeting took place in Funchal-Portugal on 30-31 March 2000, where it was decided that in order to streamline the activities of the various working groups, the country which would take over the Presidency would also be responsible for the activities of the working groups. It was also decided during this meeting that the Senior Officials would convene 3-4 times during each Presidency prior to the Ministerial Meeting.

The Eighth Ministerial Meeting took place in Tangiers on 10-11 May 2001 where deliberations focused on the Middle East Peace Process, Cooperation in the Mediterranean, Regional Integration and Investments, Promotion of the Mediterranean and Security issues in the Mediterranean.

The Ninth Ministerial Meeting took place in Mykonos/Delos-Greece on 18-19 May 2002, where for the first time the meeting was attended by intellectuals of each participating country along with some prominent international personalities such as Boutros Boutros Ghali, the ex-Secretary General of the UN. The theme of the meeting was

Dialogue of Cultures and the Code of Conduct on Terrorism was also approved and adopted during this meeting, which in itself is a very important achievement of the Forum.

III. STRUCTURE

The Mediterranean Forum is a strictly regional institution of inter-governmental dialogue. There is a rotation of the Presidency every year and at the end of each Presidency a Foreign Affairs Ministers Meeting is held.

However, there is the possibility of holding ad-hoc or Extraordinary Ministerial Meetings such as the one held in Agadir-Morocco in October 2001 on the effects of 11 September.

Senior Officials of the Mediterranean Forum hold 3-4 meetings every year. There are also expert level meetings, such as the ones on terrorism.

Seminars and workshops are held regularly on topics of common interest.

The Forum has no permanent structure such as a secretariat and the functions of a secretariat are thus performed by the coordinator of the term Presidency.

The Forum also does not have any funds, therefore all activities are catered for by the state or states wishing to engage in an activity such as a seminar or meeting.

IV. MINISTERIAL MEETINGS TO DATE

The first Ministerial Meeting was held in Alexandria-Egypt in July 1994.

This meeting was followed by; Saint-Maxime-France in April 1995; by Ravello-Italy in May 1996; by Algiers-Algeria in July 1997; by Palma de Majorca-Spain in April 1998; by Malta in March 1999; by Funchal-Portugal in March 2000; by Tangiers-Morocco in May 2001 and by Delos-Greece in May 2002.

The Mediterranean Forum has held two extraordinary sessions, in Tabarka-Tunisia in July 1995 and in Agadir-Morocco in October 2001. The Tenth ordinary meeting will take place in Antalya-Turkey on 9-10 October 2003.

V. OBJECTIVES

The eleven member countries are committed to a real, effective and comprehensive partnership in the Mediterranean area, to make this birthplace of civilisations a zone of peace and security, development and prosperity, mutual tolerance, understanding and exchanges between the peoples of the region, in the framework of the promotion of the rule of law, plural democracy and human rights.

VI. PRESIDENCY CONCLUSIONS

Alexandria-Egypt, July 1994
Saint-Maxime-France, April 1995
Ravello-Italy, May 1996
Algiers-Algeria, July 1997
Malta, March 1999
Funchal-Portugal, March 2000
Tangiers-Morocco, May 2001
Delos-Greece, May 2002
Antalya-Turkey, October 2003

For text of the Moroccan Constitution visit:
http://www.maec.gov.ma/en/default.html

Text of Morocco-EU Association Agreement in:
http://www.maec.gov.ma/en/accord_en.pdf

Euro-Mediterranean Partnership in:
http://ec.europa.eu/

Morocco-USA Free Trade Agreement:
http://www.moroccousafta.com/ftafulltext.htm

GOVERNMENT MINISTERS AND WEBSITE LINKS

Prime Minister: Mr. Abbas El Fassi
www.pm.gov.ma

Minister of State: Mr. Mohamed El Yazghi

Minister of Justice: Mr. Abdelwahed Radi
www.justice.gov.ma

Minister of Interior: Mr. Chakib Benmoussa

Minister of Foreign Affairs and Cooperation: Mr. Taieb Fassi Fihri
www.maec.gov.ma

Minister of Habous and Islamic Affairs: M. Ahmed Toufiq
www.habous.gov.ma

Secretary General of the Government: Mr. Driss Dahak
www.sgg.gov.ma

Minister in Charge of Relations with Parliament:
Mr. Mohamed Saad Alami
www.mcrp.gov.ma

Minister of Economy and Finance: Mr. Salaheddine Mezouar
www.finances.gov.ma

Minister of Transportion and Public Works: Mr. Karim Ghellab
www.mtpnet.gov.ma; www.mtmm.gov.ma

Minister of Housing and Urban Development:
M. Ahmed Taoufiq Hejira
www.mhu.gov.ma; www.matee.gov.ma

Minister of Tourism and Handicraft: Mr. Mohamed Boussaid
www.tourisme.gov.ma; www.artsenet.gov.ma

Minister of Energy, Mining, Water and Environment:
Ms. Amina Benkhadra
www.mem.gov.ma; www.minenv.gov.ma

Minister of Health: Mrs. Yasmina Baddou
www.sante.gov.ma

Minister of Youth and Sports: Ms. Nawal El Moutawakil
www.secj.gov.ma

Minister of Agriculture and Fisheries: M. Aziz Akhenouch
www.madrpm.gov.ma; www.mpm.gov.ma

Minister of Education, Higher Education, Staff Training, and Scientific Research:
Mr. Ahmed Akhchichine
www.men.gov.ma; www.alpha.gov.ma; www.dfc.gov.ma; www.cnr.ac.ma

Minister of Communication, Government Spokesman:
Mr. Khalid Naciri
www.mincom.gov.ma

Minister of Employment and Professional Training:
Mr. Jamal Aghmani
www.emploi.gov.ma

Minister of Industry, Commerce and New Technologies:
Mr. Ahmed Reda Chami
www.mcinet.gov.ma (Commerce and Industry)
www.septi.gov.ma (New Technologies)

Minister of Foreign Trade: Mr. Abdellatif Maâzouz
www.mce.gov.ma

Minister of Social Development, Family and Solidarity:
Ms. Nouzha Skalli
www.social.gov.ma; www.sefsas.gov.ma

Minister of Culture: Ms Touriya Jabrane
www.minculture.gov.ma

Minister Delegate in Charge of National Defense:
Mr. Abderrahmane Sbaï

Minister Delegate at the Prime Minister's office in charge of Economic and General Affairs:
Mr. Nizar Baraka
www.affaires-generales.gov.ma; www.invest.gov.ma

Minister Delegate at the Prime Minister's office in charge of Public Sectors' Modernization:
Mr. Mohamed Abbou
www.mmsp.gov.ma

Minister Delegate at the Prime Minister's Office in charge of Moroccan expatriates:
M. Mohammed Ameur
www.marocainsdumonde.gov.ma

Secretary of State at the Ministry of Energy, Mining, Water and Environment in charge of Water and Environment:
Mr. Abdelkébir Zahoud
www.minenv.gov.ma

Secretary of State at the Ministry of Tourism and Handicrafts in charge of handicraft Industry: Mr. Anis Birou

Secretary of State at the Ministry of Interior: Mr. Saad Hassar

Secretary of State at the Ministry of National Education, Higher Education, Staff Training, and Scientific Research in charge of Primary and Secondary Education:
Ms. Latifa Labida

Secretary of State at the Ministry of Foreign Affairs and Cooperation:
Ms. Latifa Akherbach

Secretary of State at the Ministry of Housing, Town Planning and Development in charge of Territorial Development:
Mr. Abdeslam Al Mesbahi

Trade Unions

Trade unionism was introduced into Morocco during the colonial period on the initiative of the Moroccan Communist Party. After independence, the precursor of the union action became the Moroccan Labour Union (UMT), founded in 1955.

Labour Unions

The Moroccan Labour Union (UMT); the General Union of Moroccan Workers (UGTM); the Democratic Labour Confederation (CDT); the National Union of Moroccan Workers (UNTM);the Federation of Popular Unions (USP); the Moroccan Labour Forces (FOM); the Union of Free Worker's Association (USTL); the National Popular Union (SNP); the Moroccan Workers Union (UTM); and the Democratic Syndicates Union (USD).

Teachers Union

National Union of Higher Education (SNES)

Student Unions

National Union of Moroccan Students (UNEM)
General Union of Moroccan Students (UGEM)

MOROCCO'S MAJOR RIVERS

River	Sources	Length(km)
Draa	Grand Atlas	1,200
Oum er Rbia	Middle and Grand Atlas	600
Sebou	Grand Atlas, Rif	500
Moulouya	Middle and Grand Atlas, Rif	450
Tensift	Grand Atlas	270
Ziz	Grand Atlas	270
Bouregreg	Central Massif	250

(Source: Ministry of Tourism*)*

Bilateral tax treaties signed with the following countries to avoid double taxation

	Signature	Entry into force
Denmark	08 May 1984	01 January 1992
UAE	09 February 1999	02 July 2000
Bahrain	07 April 2000	10 February 2001
Egypt	22 March 1989	21 September 1993
Lebanon	20 October 2001	07 August 2003
Germany	07 June 1972	08 October 1974
Belgium	04 May 1972	05 March 1975
Bulgaria	22 May 1996	06 December 1999
Canada	22 December 1975	09 November 1978
Spain	10 July 1978	16 May 1985
Finland	25 June 1973	01 February 1980
France	29 May 1970	05 March 1975
Italia	07 June 1972	10 March 1983
Luxembourg	19 December 1980	16 February 1984
Norway	05 May 1972	18 December 1975
Netherlands	12 August 1977	10 June 1987
Portugal	29 September 1997	27 June 2000
UK	08 September 1981	29 November 1990
Russia	12 October 1996	20 September 1999
Switzerland	31 March 1993	27 July 1995
United States	01 August 1977	30 December 1981

USEFUL LINKS

Ministry of Foreign Affairs and Cooperation : www.maec.gov.ma
Av Roosevelt- Rabat
Tel : +212 537 76 28 41/ 76 11 23
Fax : +212 537 76 55 08/ 76 46 79

Ministry of Economy and Finance : www.finances.gov.ma
Quartier Administratif, Chellah- Rabat
Tel : +212 537 76 31 71/58
Fax : +212 537 76 15 75

Ministry of Foreign Trade : www.mce.gov.ma
63, bd. Moulay Youssef – Rabat
Tel : +212 537 70 18 46/ 70 63 89
Fax : +212 537 72 71 50
E-mail : mce@mce.gov.ma

Ministry of Industry, Commerce and new Technologies : www.mcinet.gov.ma
Av. Mohammed V, Quartier administratif, Chellah- Rabat
Tel : +212 537 76 18 68/ 76 15 08
Fax : +212 537 76 62 65
E-mail : webmaster@mcinet.gov.ma

Customs and Indirect Taxes Administration : www.douane.gov.ma
Av. Annakhil, Centre des Affaires, Hay Riad- Rabat
Tel : +212 537 71 78 00/ 01
Fax : +212 537 71 78 14/ 15
E-mail : adii@douane.gov.ma

Moroccan Federation of Chambers of Commerce, Industry and Services : www.fccism.ma
6, rue Erfoud Hassan – Rabat
Tel : +212 537 76 70 51/ 78/ 81
Fax : +212 537 76 70 76

Moroccan Centre for Export Promotion : www.cmpe.org.ma
23, Rue Bnou Majed El Bahar- 20 000 – Casablanca
Tel : +212 522 30 22 10/ 30 75 88
Fax : +212 522 30 17 93/ 45 05 57
E-mail : cmpe@cmpe.org.ma

Morocco's regions, prefectures and provinces

1. Oued Eddahab-Lagouira, subdivided into:

> *1 province:* Oued Eddahab

2. Laayoune-Boujdour, subdivided into:

> *1 prefecture:* Laayoune
> *1 province:* Boujdour

3. Guelmim Es Smara, subdivided into:

> *5 provinces:* Assa-Zag, Es Smara, Guelmim, Tan-Tan, Tata

4. Souss-Massa-Draa, subdivided into:

> *5 provinces:* Ouarzazate, Zagora, Taroudant, Chtouka Ait Baha, Tiznit
> *2 prefectures:* Agadir-Ida Ou-Tanane, Inzegane-Ait Melloul

5. Gharb-Cherada-Beni Hssen, subdivided into:

> *2 provinces:* Kenitra, Sidi Kacem

6. Chaouia-Ouerdigha, subdivided into:

> *3 provinces:* Ben Slimane, Khouribga, Settat

7. Eastern Region (l'oriental), subdivided into:

> *6 provinces:* Oujda-Angad, Berkane, Taourirt, Figuig, Jerada, Nador

8. Rabat-Sale-Zemmour-Zaer, subdivided into:

> *3 prefectures*: Rabat, Sale, Skhirat-Temara
> *1 province:* Khemisset

9. Doukkala-Abda, subdivided into:

> *2 provinces:* El Jadida, Safi

10. Tadla-Azilal, subdivided into:

> *2 provinces*: Beni Mellal, Azilal

11. Meknes-Tafilalet, subdivided into:

> *2 prefectures*: Al Ismailia, Meknes-El Menzah
> *3 provinces*: El Hajeb, Ifrane, Errachidia

12. Fes-Boulemane, subdivided into:

> *3 prefectures*: Fes El Jadid-Dar Dbibegh, Fes Medina, Zouagha Moulay Yacoub
> *2 provinces*: Boulemane, Sefrou

13. Taza-El Houceima-Taounate, subdivided into:

> *3 provinces*: Al Hoceima, Taounate, Taza

14. Grand Casablanca, subdivided into:

> *8 prefectures*: Casablance-Anfa, Ain Chock-Hay Hassani, Ain-Sebaa-Hay-Mohammadi, Ben Msik-Sidi-Othmane, Sidi El Barnoussi-Zenata, El Fida-Derb Soltane, Mechouar- Casablanca, Mohammadia

15. Tangier-Tetouan, subdivided into:

> *3 prefectures*: Fahss-Bni Makada, Tangier Assila, Tetouan
> *2 provinces*: Fahss-Bni Makada, Tangier Assila, Tetouan, Chefchaouen, Larache

16. Marrakech-Tensift-El Haouz, subdivided into:

> *3 prefectures*: Marrakech-Medina, Marrakech Menara, Sidi Youssef Ben Ali
> *4 provinces*: El Kelaa Sraghna, Essaouira, Chichaoua, El Haouz

CONSULTATIVE COUNCILS (Conseils Consultatifs)

Royal Consultative Council for Saharan Affairs (Le Conseil Royal Consultatif pour les Affaires Sahariennes):
http://www.corcas.com

Consultative Council for Human Rights (Le Conseil Consultatif des Droits de l'Homme):
http://www.ccdh.org.ma

High Commission for Members of the Resistance and the Liberation Army (Le Haut Commissariat des Anciens Résistants et Membres de l'Armée de Libération):
http://www.hcar.gov.ma

High Commisssion for Planning (Le Haut Commissariat au Plan) :
http://www.hcp.ma

PUBLIC OFFICES

National Office for Research and Petroleum Exploitation (L'Office National de Recherches et d'Exploitations Pétrolières :
http://www.onarep.com

National Office for Railways (L'Office National des Chemins de Fer): http://www.oncf.ma

National Office for Electricity (L'Office National de l'Electricité):
http://www.one.org.ma

National Office for Aiports (L'Office National des Aéroports) :
http://www.onda.org.ma

Moroccan National Tourism Office (L'Office National Marocain du Tourisme):
http://81.192.52.41/onmt_FR/Marches/INS/index.aspx

Office for Industrial Development (L'Office pour le Développement Industriel):
http://www.odi.gov.ma

Office for Phosphates (L'Office Chérifien des Phosphates):
http://www.ocpgroup.ma

Regional Office for Agriculture in the Haouz Region (L'Office Régional de la Mise en Valeur Agricole du Haouz):
http://www.agriinvest-marrakech.org.ma

Office for Ports Exploitation (L'Office d'Exploitation des Ports) :
http://www.odep.org.ma

Office for Currency Exchange (L'Office des Changes):
http://www.oc.gov.ma

National Office for Fishing (L'Office National des Pêches:
http://www.onp.co.ma

National Office for Drinking Water (L'Office National de l'Eau Potable):
http://www.onep.ma

Office for Professional Training and Employment Promotion (L'Office de la Formation Professionnelle et de la Promotion du Travail):
http://www.ofppt.org.ma

Royal Air Maroc (National Airline)
www.royalairmaroc.com

FINANCIAL AND PROFESSIONAL INSTITUTIONS

Morocco's Central Bank, (Bank Al-Maghrib):
http://www.bkam.gov.ma/

Casablanca Stock Exchange (La Bourse de Casablanca):
www.casablanca-bourse.com

The Treasury (Trésorerie Générale du Royaume):
http://www.tgr.gov.ma/

National Council for Foreign Trade:
http://www.cnce.org.ma/

National Auditing Court (La Cour des Comptes):
http://www.courdescomptes.ma

The International Centre for the Promotion of Crafts (Le Centre International de Promotion de l'Artisanat:
http://www.cipa.org.ma/

Observatory for the Moroccan Economy (Le Centre Marocain de Conjoncture):
http://www.techno.net.ma/cmc

Confederation of Moroccan Industry (Confédération Générale des Entreprises du Maroc):
http://www.cgem.ma

Moroccan Centre for Promotion of Exports (Le Centre Marocain de Promotion des Exportations):
http://www.cmpe.org.ma

National Centre for Documentation (Le Centre National de la Documentation):
http://www.cnd.hcp.ma

National Agency Against Unacceptable Housing (L'Agence Nationale de Lutte contre l'Habitat Insalubre):
http://www.anhi.ma

National Committee for the Prevention of Road Accidents (Comité National de Prévention des Accidents de la Circulation):
http://www.cnpac.ma

Morocco's Highways (Autoroutes du Maroc):
http://www.adm.ma

National Agency for Telecommunications Regulation (L'Agence Nationale de Réglementation des Télécommunications):
http://www.anrt.net.ma

National Deposit and Management Agency for Retirement Funds (Caisse de Dépôt et de Gestion):
http://www.cdg.org.ma

Moroccan Retirement Fund (Caisse Marocaine des Retraites:
http://www.cmr.gov.ma

National Social Security Fund (Caisse Nationale de la Sécurité Sociale): http://www.cnss.org.ma

Centre for Development of Renewable Energy (Centre de Développement des Energies Renouvelables):
http://www.cder.org.ma/

National Centre for Coordination and Planning of Scientific and Technical Research (Le Centre National de Coordination et de Planification de la Recherche Scientifique et Technique):
http://www.cnr.ac.ma/acceuil.htm

Agency for Urban and Preservation of Fez (Agence Urbaine et de Sauvegarde de Fès):
http://www.ausf.org.ma

Casablanca Chambre of Commerce, Industry and Services (Chambre de Commerce, d'Industrie, et de Services de Casablanca:
http://www.ccisc.gov.ma

Post Office (Barid Al-Maghrib) (La Poste):
http://www.poste.ma

Customs and indirect taxation (Administration des Douanes et Impôts Indirects):
http://www.douane.gov.ma/

International Finance Corporation – IFC
8, Rue Kamal Mohamed – 2eme etage – 20000 Casablanca Phone: 212 522 48 46 86 Fax: 212 522 48 46 90

International Finance Corporation – IFC
8, Rue Kamal Mohamed – 2eme etage – 20000 Casablanca Phone: 212 522 48 46 86 Fax: 212 522 48 46 90

Casablanca Regional Investment Centre
www.casainvest.ma

INTERNATIONAL ORGANISATIONS

Arab-Maghreb Union Secretariat
26, Rue Oqba – Agdal – Rabat Phone: 212 537 77 26 72
Fax: 212 537 77 26 93.http://www.maghrebarabe.org

Jerusalem Fund (Bayt Mal Al-Qods Acharif):
http://www.bma-alqods.org

The Islamic Educational, Scientific and Cultural Organization (ISESCO) : http://www.isesco.org.ma

Islamic Centre for development and Commerce
Tour des Habous, Avenue dea Far, B.P. 13545, Casablanca
Tel: 00 212 522314974 Fax 00 212 522310110
email: icdt@icdt.org Website: www.icdt.org

Arab League Educational, Cultural and Scientific Organization
82, Zankat Oued Ziz, Agdal,Rabat
Phone: 212 537 77 24 22 Fax: 212 537 77 24 26

Arab Industrial Development and Mining Organisation – OADIM
BP 8019, UN 10102, Rabat.
Phone: 212 537 77 26 00 Fax: 212 537 77 21 88

Delegation of the Commission of the European Communities
2 Bis, Avenue de Meknes – B.P. 1302 – Rabat Phone: 212 537 76 12
17 Fax: 212 537 76 11 56

Organisation of The Islamic Conference – OIC
Islamic Educational, Scientific and Cultural Organization - ISESCO
Avenue Attine – Hay Riad – B.P. 2275-10104 – Rabat Phone: 212 537
71 53 05 Fax: 212 537 77 20 58 E-mail: webmaster@isesco.org.ma
Web: www.isesco.ma.

Islamic Development Bank
177, Avenue John Kennedy – Souissi – B.P. 5003 – Rabat Phone: 212
537 75 71 91 Fax: 212 537 75 72 60

MEDIA INSTITUTIONS

There are 18 dailies and 24 Weeklies in Arabic and French. There are also numerous monthly and quarterly publications The following are the main publications:

AL MASSAE
Independent Arabic daily
Website: http://www.almassae.com
Email: contact@almassae.press.ma

AL-AHDATH AL MAGHRIBIA
Independent Arabic daily
Website: www.ahdath.info
Address: 5 Rue Saint Emilion, Hay La Jironde - Casablanca
Phone: 00 212 52244 30 38/45/70/71

AL-ALAM
Arabic daily of the Istiqlal Party (PI).
Website: www.Alalam.ma
Email: journal@alalam.ma
Address: Avenue Hassan II, Lotissement Vita -Rabat
Phone: 00 212 537 29 26 42/44 – 037 29 29 93 – 037 29 02 08
Fax: 00 212 537 29 17 84

AL-ITTIHAD AL ICHTIRAKI
Arabic daily of the Socialist Union for the Popular Forces (l'Union Socialiste des Forces Populaires (USFP).
Website: www.alittihad.press.ma
Email: ail@menara.ma
Address: 33 Avenue Amir Abdelkader, B.P 2165 – Casabalanca
Phone: 00 212 522 61 94 00 à 04 – 022 62 32 32
Fax: 00 212 522 61 94 05 – 022 62 28 10

AN-NAHAR AL-MAGHRIBIA
Independent Arabic daily
Website: www.annahar.ma

Email: annahar21@yahoo.fr
annaharalmaghribia@menara.ma
Address: 12 Place Alaouiene, 2ème étage, appt 4 - Rabat
Phone: -00 212 537 73 75 68 – 037 70 24 81
Fax: 00 212 537 73 75 47 – 037 70 24 33

AS-SABAH
Independent Arabic daily
Website: www.assabah.press.ma
Email: assabah@assabah.press.ma
Address: 70 Avenue El Massira Al Khadra - Casablanca
Phone : 00 212 522 95 36 60
Fax : 00 212 522 36 43 58

BAYANE AL-YOUM
Arabic daily of the Party for Progress and Socialsm (Parti du Progrès
et du Socialisme) (PPS)
Website: www.bayanealyaoume.ma
Email: albayane@casanet.net.ma
Address: 119 Avenue Emile Zola - Casabalanca
Phone: 00 212 522 30 76 66
Fax: 00 212 522 30 80 80

ALHARAKA
Arabic daily of the Popular Movement (Mouvemnt Populaire)
http://harakamp.org.ma

AL-BAYANE
French daily of the Party for Progress and Socialsm (Parti du Progrès
et du Socialisme) (PPS).
Website: www.albayane.ma
Email: albayane@casanet.net.ma
Adresse: 119,bd Emile Zola, 8éme étage, B.P 13152 - Casablanca
Phone : 00 212 522 30 76 66 - 022 44 99 79 - 022 30 78 82
Fax : 00 212 522 44 25 49

L'OPINION
French daily of the Istiqlal Party (PI).
Website: www.lopinion.ma
Email: lopinion@lopinion.ma
Address: Avenue Hassan II, Lotissement Vita - Rabat
Phone: 00 212 537 29 30 02 /03/ 04/ 06 - 037 29 29 92
Fax: 00 212 537 29 39 97

LE MATIN DU SAHARA ET DU MAGHREB
French daily
Website: www.lematin.ma
Address: 17, Rue Othman Ben Affan - Casablanca
Phone: 00 212 522 48 91 00
Fax: 00 212 522 26 29 69

AUJOURD'HUI LE MAROC
Independent French daily
Website: www.aujourdhui.ma
Email: alm@aujourdhui.ma
Address: 213, Rond Point d'Europe - Casablanca
Phone: 00 212 522 26 26 74
Fax: 00 212 522 26 24 43

LIBERATION
French daily of the Socialist Union for the Popular Forces (l'Union
Socialiste des Forces Populaires (USFP)
Website: www.liberation.press.ma
Email: liberation@usfp.ma
Address: 33, Rue Amir Abdelkader, BP 2165 - Casablanca
Phone: 00 212 522 61 94 00 à 05 - 022 62 32 32 - 022 61 34 46
Fax 00 212 522 62 09 72

L'ECONOMISTE
Business independent French daily
Website: www.leconomiste.com
Email: info@leconomiste.com
Address: 70, Boulevard El Massira Al Khadra - Casablanca
Phone : 00 212 522 95 36 00 Fax : 00 212 522 36 59 26

LA GAZETTE DU MAROC
Independent French weekly current affairs magazine
Website: www.lagazettedumaroc.com
Email: redaction@lagazettedumaroc.com
Addess: 58 avenue des Far, Tour des Habous 13ème étage - Casablanca
Phone : 00 212 522 54 81 50 à 52
Fax : 00 212 522 31 80 94

LE JOURNAL HEBDOMADAIRE
Independent French weekly current affairs magazine
Website : http://www.lejournal-press.com
Email : courrier@lejournal-hebdo.com
Addess : 61, Avenue Des Far 20000 - Casablanca
Phone : 00 212 522 54 66 70 / 71
Fax : 00 212 522 44 61 85

MAROC HEBDO INTERNATIONAL
Independent French weekly current affairs magazine
Website: www.maroc-hebdo.com
Email: mhi@maroc-hebdo.press.ma
Address: 4, Rue des Flamants Riviera - Casablanca
Phone: 00 212 522 23 81 76 à79
Fax : 00 212 522 98 21 61 - 022 98 13 46

LA NOUVELLE TRIBUNE
Independent French weekly current affairs magazine
Website: www.lanouvelletribune.com
Email: courrier@lanouvelletribune.com
redaction@lanouvelletribune.com
Address: 320 Bd Zerktouni - Casablanca
Phone: 00 212 522 42 46 70
Fax: 00 212 522 20 00 31

NICHANE
Independent Arabic weekly current affairs magazine
Website: www.aljareeda.ma
Email: aljareedaalukhra@yahoo.com
Address : 28 Avenue des Far - Casablanca
Phone: 00212 522 22 19 18
Fax : 00 212 522 22 22 13 or 00 212 522 22 20 97

AL-AYAM
Independent weekly Arabic current affairs newspaper
Website : www.alayam.ma
Email : alayam@menara.com
Address: Place Baki, Angle Avenue Mohammed V et Rue Mohamed
Smiha 508, 5ème étage - Casablanca
Phone : 00 212 522 44 19 72 – 022 44 26 94 – 022 44 20 08
Fax : 00 212 522 44 11 73

LE REPORTER
Independent French weekly current affairs magazine
Website: www.lereporter.ma
Email: lereporter@menara.ma
Address: 1, Sahat Al Istiqlal 2éme étage - Casablanca
Phone: 00 212 522 54 11 03/04
Fax: 00 212 522 54 11 05

TEL QUEL
Independent French weekly current affairs magazine
Website: www.telquel-online.com
Email: courrier@telquel.info
Address: 28 Avenue des Far - Casablanca
Phone: 00 212 522 22 09 51
Fax : 00 212 522 22 05 63 or 00 212 522 22 09 64

LA VERITE
Independent French Weekly current affairs newspaper
Website: www.laverite.ma
Address: 174 Bd Zerktouni, 6ème ètage - Casablanca
Phone: 00 212 522 20 64 11/32 Fax: 00 212 522 20 64 23

LA VIE ECONOMIQUE
Independent Fench weekly newspaper for business and finance
Website: www.lavieeco.com
Email: redaction@lavieeco.ma
Addess: 5 Boulevard Allal Ben Yacine - Casablanca
Phone : 00 212 522 44 46 26 - 022 44 38 68/69

AT-TAJDID
Arabic Weekly for the Movement of Unification and Refom
(Mouvement de l'Unification et de la Réforme (MUR).
Website : www.attajdid.ma
Email : attajdid@attajdid.ma
Address : 3 Avenue La Résidence, Hay L'Ocean 10000 - Rabat
Phone : 00 212 537 70 58 54 – 037 20 76 44
Fax : 00 212 537 70 58 52 – 037 20 83 66

Moroccan National Press Union (Syndicat National de la Presse Marocaine):
http://www.snpm.ma/
27 avenue Prince Moulay Abdellah- Rabat,
Tel : +212 537 70 30 77,
Fax : +212 537 70 93 31

High Authority for Audiovisual Media (Haute Autorite de la Communication Audiovisuelle):
http://www.haca.ma
Espace les palmiers, Lot 26, Angle Avenues Anakhil et Mehdi Ben Barka, B.P 20590 - Hay Ryad Rabat
Tel: +212 537 57 96 00
Email: info@haca.ma

Moroccan Bureau for Copy Right (Bureau Marocain du Droit d'Auteur):
http://www.bmda.org.ma,
6,Rue mohamed Jazouli BP RABAT
Tél : +212 537 72 21 97
Fax : +212 537 73 26 40

TV and Radio Advertising Company (Regie3):
http://www.regie3.ma/
37, Bd Abdellatif Ben Kaddour, Casablanca
tel.: 00 212 5 22 95 02 80
Fax: 00 212 5 22 39 56 70
E-mail: regie3@regie3.ma

Public Advertising Company (Service Autonome de Publicite) (SAP):
http://www.sap.ma/

Moroccan internet Portal and Internet Provider part of Maroc Telecom:
http://www.menara.ma
National News Agency (Maghreb Arabe Presse):
www.map.ma/fr
22, Avenue Allal Ben Abdellah B.P. 1049 - Rabat – 10000
Tel: +212 537 27 94 00
E-mail: mapweb@map.co.ma

(SOREAD):
http://www.2m.tv/
Km 7.3 route de Rabat, Aïn Sebaâ 20250 Casablanca
Tel: +212 522 66 73 73/00
E-mail: portail@tv2m.co.ma

National Company for Radio and Television (Société Nationale de Radiodiffusion et de Télévision) (SNRT):
http://www.snrt.ma/
1, Rue El Blihi- B.P. 1042- Rabat
Tel : +212 537 76 68 85

Radio Mediterranee Internationale:
http://www.medi1.com/
35, rue Lamsallah- B.P. 2055- Tangier
Tel : +212 539 93 65 95
Fax : +212 539 93 63 63
E-mail : med1@med1.com

Institut Superieur de l'Information et de la Communication (ISIC):
www.isic.ma, B.P.6205 Madinat Al Irfane Rabat Maroc
Tel: +212 537 77 33 40/55
Fax: +212 537 77 27 89
E-mail: contact@isic.ma

Moroccan Association of Newspapers Publishers (Association Marocaine des Editeurs de Journaux)
201, Boulevard de Bordeaux, Casablanca, Maroc
Tel. : +212 22.27.16.50
Fax : +212 22.29.72.85 / 22.40.40.16.

Association of Moroccan publishers (Association Marocaine des Editeurs)
34, Bd Victor Hugo -Casablanca
Tel.: 022 30 23 75
Fax : 022 30 65 11
201, Boulevard de Bordeaux, Casablanca, Maroc
Tel. : +212 22.27.16.50
Fax : +212 22.29.72.85 / 22.40.40.16

PRESS DISTRIBUTORS

SOCHESPRESS
Rue Rahal Ben Ahmed – ex Dinant, ang.St Saëns,
20300 Casablanca. Adresse Postale : BP : 13683, 20001 Casablanca .
Phone: 00 212 522 40 02 23 Fax: 00 212 522 40 40 31
E-mail: dispresse1@sochepress.ma

SAPRESS
70, Rue Sijilmassa, Casablanca.
Phone 00 212 522249200
Fax: 00 212 522 24 92 14
Website: sapress.ma

SOMADED
88, Bd Mohammed V, Casablanca.
Phone 212 522 26 88 60

AL AOULA

AL AOULA SATELLITAIRE

TV LAÂYOUNE

2M
2M SATELLITAIRE

ARRIYADIA

ARRABIÂ

AL MAGHRIBIYA

ASSADISSA

AFLAM TV

MEDI 1 SAT

2M RADIO
http://www.radio2m.fm

RADIO NATIONALE
http://www.snrt.ma

RADIO AMAZIGH
http://www.snrt.ma

RABAT CHAÎNE INTER
http://www.snrt.ma

RADIO MOHAMMED VI DU SAINT CORAN
http://www.snrt.ma

RADIO CASA FM
http://www.snrt.ma

RADIO RÉGIONALE D'AGADIR
http://www.snrt.ma

RADIO RÉGIONALE DE CASABLANCA
http://www.snrt.ma

RADIO RÉGIONALE DE DAKHLA
http://www.snrt.ma

RADIO RÉGIONALE DE FÈS
http://www.snrt.ma

RADIO RÉGIONALE DE LAÂYOUNE
http://www.snrt.ma

RADIO RÉGIONALE DE MARRAKECH
http://www.snrt.ma

RADIO RÉGIONALE DE MEKNÈS
http://www.snrt.ma

RADIO RÉGIONALE D'OUJDA
http://www.snrt.ma

RADIO RÉGIONALE DE TANGER
http://www.snrt.ma

RADIO RÉGIONALE DE TETOUAN
http://www.snrt.ma

RADIO MEDI 1
www.medi1.com

RADIO SAWA
www.radiosawa.com

RADIO ATLANTIC
www.atlanticradio.ma

www.hitradio.ma

ASWAT
www.aswat.ma

MFM ATLAS

MFM SAISS

MFM SOUSS

www.chadafm.net

www.radioplus.ma

CHADA FM

RADIO PLUS MARRAKECH

CAP RADIO

www.capradio.ma

RADIO PLUS AGADIR

www.radioplus.ma

TRADE ASSOCIATIONS AND EDERATIONS

Confederation of Industry and entreprises (Confederation Generale des Entreprises du Maroc) (CGEM.)
Angle Avenue des FAR, rue Mohamed Errachdi - Casablanca
Tel. : 00 212 522 25 26 96/97/98/99
Fax : 00 212 522 25 38 39
Telex: 23835
E-mail : cgem@mail.cbi.net.ma

Association of Information Technology Professionals (Association des Professionnels des Technologies de l'Information) (APEBI)
17, rue Najib Mahfoud, Place Ollier, Gautier - Casablanca.
Tel : 00 212 522 27 47 57.
Fax : 00 212 522 27 47 28

Moroccan Association of Textiles and Clothing Industry (Association Marocaine des Industries du Textile et de l'Habillement) (A.M.I.T.H.)
92, Bd My Rachid,- Casablanca
Tel. : 00 212 522 94 20 84/94 03 86
Fax : 00 212 522 94 03 87

Association of Moroccan Advertisers (Groupement des Annonceurs du Maroc)
23, rue Jean Jaures, Gauthier - Casablanca
Tel. : 00 212 522 26 98 39
Fax : 00 212 522 20 34 41
Email : gam@casanet.net.ma

Association of Flowers Producers and Exporters (Association des Producteurs Exportateurs de Fleurs) (a.m.p.e.x.fleurs)
9, avenue Khalid Ibn Alwalid - Casablanca
Tel.:00 212 522 35 55 55/25 26 96
Fax: 00 212 522 35 33 98

Moroccan Association of Pharmaceutical Industry (Association Marocaine de l'Industrie Pharmaceutique) (a.m.i.p.)

Place Division Leclerc-bd. Abderrahim Bouabid - Oasis, Imm. Amir
1er etage- Casablanca
Tel. : 00 212 522 23 36 90 / 022 23 44 45
Fax : 00 212 522 23 40 90
Email : amip@iam.net.ma

Moroccan Association of experters (Association Marocaine des Exportateurs) (a.s.m.e.x.)
36, bd. D'Anfa residence anafe- Casablanca
Tel. : 00 212 522 26 10 33 / 022 22 15 / 022 29 65 84/94
Fax : 00 212 522 39 58 94
E-mail : asmex@asmex.org
Site Web : http://www.asmex.org

Association of Moroccan Mining Industry (Association des Industries Minieres du Maroc) (A.I.M.M.)
1, place Istiqlal – 3eme Etage - Casablanca
Tel. : 00 212 522 30 68 98
Fax : 00 212 522 31 99 96

Association of Maritime brokers (Association des Agents Maritimes Consignataires du Maroc)
Tel. : 00 212 522 45 98 94
Fax : 00 212 522 30 49 38

Association of Information Technology Professionals (Association des Professionnels de l'Informatique de la Bureautique et de la Telematique) (a.p.e.b.i.)
Place Zellaqa Tour Atlas – 2eme Etage - Casablanca
Tel. : 00 212 522 30 85 85 / 30 91 11
Fax : 00 212 522 30 00 30

Moroccan Association for Motoring Industry and Commerce (Association Marocaine pour l'Industrie et le Commerce de l'Automobile) (a.m.i.c.a)
625, boulevard Mohammed V – 5eme etage - Casablanca
Tel. : 00 212 522 24 28 82
Fax: 00 212 522 24 85 81

Association of Petroleum Companies in Morocco (Groupement des Petroliers du Maroc)
42, Rue Imam Mousline Naphte club-oasis-Casablanca
Tel.: 00 212 522 99 09 50 / 98 32 77
Fax: 00 212 522 99 17 51

Moroccan Union of High Sea Fishing (Union Marocaine de la Peche Hauturiere) (u.m.a.p.)
Tel : 00 212 528 84 60 69
Fax : 00 212 528 84 60 86

Central Committee for Moroccan owners of fishing trawlers (Comite Central des Armateurs Marocains)
7, Bd de la resistance -Casablanca
Tel. : 00 212 522 30 30 12
Fax: 00 212 522 30 49 38

Moroccan Federation of Insurance and Reinsurance (Federation Marocaine des Societes d'Assurance et de Reassurance) (f.m.s.a.r.)
83, AV. des FAR -Casablanca
Tel. : 00 212 522 31 07 51/31 48 50/31 01 53
Fax : 00 212 522 31 14 57/31 31 37

Federation of canned agricultural products Industry (Federation des Industries de la Conserve des Produits Agricoles du Maroc) (F.I.C.O.P.A.M.)
77, Rue Mohamed Smiha - Casablanca
Tel. : 00 212 522 30 97 62
Fax : 00 212 522 30 35 34

Federation of Chemical Industries (Federation des Industries Chimiques) (F.I.C.)
Tel.: 00 212 522 26 11 40
Fax: 00 212 522 35 41 65

National Federation of Hotel Industries (Federation Nationale de l'Industrie Hoteliere) (F.N.I.H.)
Place Zellaqa - Tour Atlas – 3eme etage - Casablanca
Tel. : 00 212 522 27 27 25 / 26 Fax : 00 212 522 39 11 36

National Federation of Insurance Brokers (Federation Nationale des Agents et Courtiers d'Assurance au Maroc)
1, Avenue de l'Armee Royale - Casablanca
Tel. : 00 212 522 26 19 78
Fax : 00 212 522 26 19 82

Moroccan Federation of Leather Industries (Federation Marocaine des Industries du Cuir) (f.e.d.i.c.)
50, Rue Tata, Casablanca 20 000
Tel. : 00 212 522 22 77 16/ 22 71 02
Fax : 00 212 522 22 72 99
Site web : www.fedic.org.ma
E-mail : fedic@menara.ma

Federation of Metalical, Mechanical and Electrical Industries (Federation des Industries Metallurgiques, Mecaniques et Electriques du Maroc) (F.I.M.M.E)
147, rue Mohamed Smiha - Casablanca
Tel. : 00 212 522 30 20 34 / 30 16 83
Fax : 00 212 522 31 99 96

Federation of Travel Agencies in Morocco (Federation des Agences de Voyage du Maroc)
10 Rue El Oraibi JILALI-casablanca
Tel. : 00 212 522 26 03 00
Fax : 00212 522 27 79 63

Moroccan Confederation of Small Entreprises (Confédération Marocaine de la Jeune Entreprise)

16 Rue Zalaghe Agdal - Rabat
Email : cmje@microbit.net.ma

Federation of Agricultural Chambers in Morocco (Federation des Chambres d'Agriculture du Maroc)

2, Rue Ghandi-Rabat
Tel : +212 537 70 69 29
Fax : +212 537 70 69 22

Federation of European Union Chambers of Commerce
Tour Atlas, Place Zallaqa. – Casablanca

Tel : +212 522 45 03 00
Fax : +212 522 45 04 45

German Chamber of Commerce and Industry

8, rue Khouribga – Casablanca
Tel : +212 522 44 98 22/23
Fax : +212 522 44 96 93

American Chamber of Commerce and Industry
c/o Holday Inn – Casablanca

Tel : +212 522 29 49 49
Fax : +212 522 49 18 80

Belgo-Luxembourgian Chamber of Commerce and Industry

124, Avenue Moulay Hassan Ier - Casablanca
Tel : +212 522 20 00 61
Fax : +212 522 20 33 83

Spanish Chamber of Commerce and Industry

6, Rue Hsaine Ramadan (Ex-rue de l'Eglise)- Casablanca
Tel : +212 522 30 56 02
15, Avenue Mers Sultan- Casablanca
Fax : +212 522 30 31 65

French Chamber of Commerce and Industry
Tel : +212 522 22 23 99
Fax : +212 522 20 01 30
E-mail : cfcim@techno.net.ma

Italian Chamber of Commerce and Industry
Rue Amine Kacem – Casablanca
Tel : +212 522 27 82 17
Fax : +212 522 27 86 27

Swiss Chamber of Commerce and Industry
305, Boulevard Bir Anzarote – Romandie II Appt No 4- Casablanca
Tel : +212 522 36 27 93 Fax : +212 522 36 49 66

British Chamber of Commerce and Industry
65, Avenue Hassan Sghir- Casablanca 20 000
Tel : +212 522 44 88 65/60/61
Fax : +212 522 44 88 68
E-mail : britcham@techno.net.ma

Association of Importers of Milk and Canned Food (Association des Importeurs de Lait et de Conserve
Tel : +212 522 36 96 86
Fax : +212 522 30 01 13

Professional Association of producers of perfums and Cosmetics (Association Professionnelle des Fabricants de Parfumerie et de Cosmetique au Maroc) (P.A.R.F.U.M.A)
27, Rue Verdi- Casablanca
Tel : +212 522 24 01 61
Fax : +212 522 24 70 71

Moroccan Association of Importers and Distributors of Chemical Products (Association Marocaine des Importateurs-Distributeurs de Produits Chimiques)
36, Rue Chaouia, Casablanca
Tel : +212 522 22 92 15
Fax : +212 522 27 42 74

Association of Importers of Agricultural Machinery (Association des Marchants Importateurs de Materiel Agricole (A.M.I.M.A)
23, Bd Mohammed Abdou- c/o CGEM – Casablanca
Tel : +212 522 22 41 74
Fax : +212 522 30 60 82

Professional Association of Importers of Heavy Machinery (Association Professionnelle des Importateurs de Materiel) (A.P.I.M)
23, Bd Mohammed Abdou- c/o CGEM – Casablanca
Tel : +212 522 25 26 96
Fax : +212 522 24 50 83

Association of Transit Brokers certified by Customs (Association des Transitaires Agrées en Douane au Maroc)
74, Rue Mohammed SMIHA, - Casablanca
Tel : +212 522 30 03 30
Fax : +212 522 30 11 86

Professional Association of Sellers of Electrical Equipment (Association Professionnelle des Marchands de Materiel Electriques)
Tel : +212 522 27 50 82
Fax : +212 522 24 50 83

Groupement Industriel des Commercants d'Electronique
Tel : +212 522 30 15 42
Fax : +212 522 30 33 03

Professional Association of Importers of Wood in Morocco (Association Professionnelle des Importateurs de Bois au Maroc) (A.P.I.B.M.)
82, Rue Bachir AL IBRAHIMI- Casablanca
Tel : +212 522 30 03 96
Fax : +212 522 40 03 44

Professional Association of Master Printers (Association Professionnelle des Maitres Imprimeurs)
Tel : +212 522 60 25 82
Fax : +212 522 60 37 68

Association of Transporters of Paper (Association des Transformateurs de Papier)
Tel : +212 522 24 25 08
Fax : +212 522 24 25 09

Professional Association of Ceramic Industry (Association Professionnelle de l'industrie céramique)
Tel : +212 528 35 50 72
Fax : +212 528 33 50 38

Association of Car Importers (Association des importateurs de Vehicules Automobiles Montes (A.I.V.A.M)
Bd Corniche- c/o Univers Motors
Tel : +212 522 31 76 04
Fax : +212 522 39 13 31

Association of Property developers in Morocco (Association des Lotisseurs et Promoteurs Immobiliers du Maroc) (A.L.P.I.M)
29, av. Lalla Yacout- c/o Fiduver- Casablanca
Tel : +212 522 31 74 47
Fax : +212 522 30 34 64

Association of Metal Sellers (Association des Marchands de Fer du Maroc)
Tel : +212 522 27 50 82
Fax : +212 522 24 37 34

Moroccan Federation of Consultant engineers (Federation Marocaine du Conseil de l'Ingenierie)
Tel : +212 537 75 61 01
Fax : +212 537 75 61 00

Moroccan Association of Auditors (Association Marocaine des Auditeurs Consultants Internes) (A.M.A.C.I)
175, bd. Mohammed Zerktouni-c/o ODEP- Casablanca
Tel : +212 522 23 23 24
Fax : +212 522 25 78 85

Association of Property Developers (Association des Promoteurs Immobiliers)
Tel/Fax : +212 539 93 47 16

Association of Exporters of Cork (Association des Exportateurs Industriels en Liege du Maroc)
Tel : +212 522 36 50 42
Fax : +212 537 85 42 20

Association of Young Entrepreneurs in the Souss Region (Association des Jeunes Entrepreneurs et Promoteurs du Souss) (A.J.P.E.S)
Tel : +212 528 31 40 80
Fax : +212 528 31 23 91

Association of Marble Industry (Association des Marbriers du Maroc)
Tel : +212 522 39 43 13
Fax : +212 522 39 43 15

National Association of Private Clinics (Association Nationale des Cliniques Privées)
105, bd. Zerktouni – Casablanca
Tel : +212 522 29 90 19
Fax : +212 522 20 34 88

National Association of Producers of Flour and fish oil (Association Nationale des Fabricants de Farine et d'Huile de Poisson)
Tel : +212 528 84 60 19/82 36 09
Fax : +212 528 84 60 19

Moroccan Association of Wine Producers (Association Marocaine des Semouliers)
Tel : +212 522 35 45 63
Fax : +212 522 35 47 51

Association of Rabat and Kenitra Hotel Industry (Association de l'Industrie Hôtelière de Rabat et Kenitra)
Tel : +212 537 70 70 30
Fax : +212 537 70 63 54

Association of Fez Hotel Industry (Association de l 'Industrie Hôtelière de Fès)
Tel : +212 535 65 22 30
Fax : +212 535 65 19 17

National Federation of Construction and Public Works (Federation Nationale de Batiment et de Travaux Publics (F.N.B.T.P.)
432, Rue Mostapha El Maani- Casablanca
Tel : +212 522 20 02 69
Fax : +212 522 48 32 74

Federation of Indutrial Sea Products (Federation Industrielle des Produits de la Mer)
Boulevard Prince Moulay Abdellah- Immeuble A 1er etage –
Appartement 15- B.P.186, Casablanca
Tel : +212 528 82 36 09
Fax : +212 528 84 60 19

Federation of of canned industries in morocco (Federation des Industries de la Conserve du Maroc) (F.I.C.O.M.A)
Quartier Longchamp- 7 rue No 5- Casablanca
Tel : +212 522 36 50 42
Fax : +212 522 36 61 54

Federation of Small and Medium Entreprises (Federation des PME et PMI)

Angle Av. des FAR et rue Mohammed Errachid- Casablanca
Tel : +212 522 25 26 96
Fax : +212 522 25 38 39
E-mail : cgem@mail.cbi.net.ma

Professional Association for Commercial and Technical Training (Association Professionnelle de l'Enseignement Commercial et Technique)

218, Bd. Zerktouni- Casablanca
Tel : +212 522 26 59 67
Fax : +212 522 40 54 13

Association for the Promotion of Research and Administrative Studies (Association pour la Promotion des Recherches et Etudes Administratives)

B.P. 1076- Rabat
Tel : +212 537 77 57 17
Fax : +212 537 77 07 80

Moroccan Association of Private Teaching Institutions (Association Marocaine des Etablissements d'enseignement Professionnel Prive) (AMEP)

89, Rue Abou Al Aala Zahar- Quartier des Hopitaux, Casablanca
Tel : +212 522 80 01 32
Fax : +212 522 80 01 02

Federation of Chambers of Commerce and Industry

56, Avenue de France, Agdal, Rabat
Phone: 212 537 76 65 23/24

Federation of Chambers of Handicrafts

27 Avenue Pasteur, Rabat
Phone: 212 53 77 3 39 55

FOREIGN EMBASSIES IN MOROCCO

Afghanistan
EMBASSY: Non resident
32, Avenue Raphaël 75, 116 Paris,France
Phone: 0033 145 25 05 29; Fax: 0033 145 24 60 68

Albania
EMBASSY: Non resident
64-5B 28006, - Madrid, Spain
Phone: 91 562 69 85; Fax: 91 561 37 75

Algeria
EMBASSY: **RABAT**
46, AV. Tarik Ibn Ziyad, Rabat;
Phone: +212 537 66 15 74 Fax: +212 57 76 22 37
CONSULATE GENERAL: **CASABLANCA**
159, Bd, Moulay Idrissi 1er, Casablanca-
Phone: +212 522 86 41 75 Fax: +212 522 86 02 53
CONSULATE: **OUJDA**
11,Boulevard de Taza, BP444, Oujda
Phone: 212 56 71 04 52 Fax: 212 56 71 04 16

Angola
EMBASSY: **RABAT**
Ahmed Rifaï, Km 5, Souissi - Rabat B.P. 1318
Phone: 212 537 65 92 39; Fax: 212 537 65 92 38 / 212 37 65 37 03
E-mail: amb.angola@menara.ma

Argentina
EMBASSY: **RABAT**
4 Rue Mehdi Ben Barka, Souissi, Rabat
Phone: 212 537 75 51 20; Fax: 212 537 75 54 10

Australia
EMBASSY: Non resident
4, Rue jean Rey, 75015 Paris - FRANCE

Phone: 331 40 59 33 00; Fax: 0033 1 40 59 33 10

Austria
EMBASSY: **RABAT**
2, Zankat Tiddas - B.P. 135 - RABAT
Phone: 212 537 76 40 03; Fax: 212 537 76 54 25
E-mail: rabat-ob@bmeia.gv.at

Azerbaijan
EMBASSY: Non resident
3, Rue Abou Hanifa, Agdal - RABAT
Phone: 212 537 67 19 15; Fax: 212 537 67 19 18

Bahrain
EMBASSY: **RABAT**
KM 6.7 Route des Zaers,Rue Beni Hassan villa 318 quartier des
ambassadeurs, Souissi, Rabat
Phone: 212 57 63 35 00; Fax: 212 537 63 07 32
E-mail: ambassadeurbh@menara.ma

Bangladesh
EMBASSY: **RABAT**
25, Avenue Tarek Ibn Ziad - Rabat
Phone: 212 537 76 67 31; Fax: 212 537 76 67 29
E-mail: bdoot@mtds.com
Web page: www.bangladeshembassy-morocco.org

Belgium
EMBASSY: **RABAT**
6, AVENUE DE MOHAMMED EL FASSI HASSAN - RABAT
Phone: 212 537 26 80 60; Fax: 212 537 76 70 03;
E-mail: rabat@diplobel.be
Web page: www.diplomatie.be/rabat
CONSULATE GENERAL: **CASABLANCA**
9, Rue Al Farabi 20 000 - CASABLANCA
Phone: 212 22 43 17 80; Fax: 212 22 22 07 22
E-mail: casablanca@diplobel.be
Web page: www.diplomatie.be/casablanca

CONSULATE: **TANGER**
41, BD Mohamed V, Residence AL-Waha (2ème ETAGE)- Tanger
Phone: 212 539 94 11 30; Fax: 212 539 94 11 30

Benin
EMBASSY: RABAT
30, Avenue mehdi ben barka - B.P. 5187 - 10105, Souissi Rabat
Phone: 212 537 75 41 58; Fax: 212 537 75 41 56
E-mail: benin@menara.ma

Bolivia
EMBASSY: Non resident
VELAZQUEZ, 26 3°A 28001 Madrid - ESPAGNE
Phone: 34 91 578 08 35; Fax: 34 91 577 39 46

Bosnia and Herzegovina
EMBASSY: Non resident
C/Lagasca, 24,2°Izqda - Madrid
Phone: 0034 91 57 50 87 0; Fax: 0034 91 43 55 05 6

Brazil
EMBASSY: RABAT
10, Avenue El Jacaranda -Secteur 2 Hay Riad- 10000 Rabat
Phone: 212 537 71 46 13; Fax: 212 537 71 48 08
E-mail: ambassadedubresil@menara.ma

Brunei-Darussalam
EMBASSY: Non resident
19, Rue Ahmed Rifaï -Souissi -Rabat
Phone: 212 537 65 31 43; Fax: 212 537 65 31 65
E-mail: enbdr88@iam.net.ma

Bulgaria
EMBASSY: **RABAT**
4, Avenue Ahmed El Yazidi, Rabat - B.P. 10000
Phone: 212 537 76 54 77; Fax: 212 537 76 32 01
E-mail: bulemrab@yahoo.com

Burkina Faso
EMBASSY: **RABAT**
7, Rue Al Bousiri - Agdal; B.P 6484 -10101, Rabat
Phone: 212 537 67 55 12; Fax: 212 537 67 55 17

Cameroon
EMBASSY: **RABAT**
20, Rue du Rif - Souissi - B.P. 1790 - Rabat
Phone : 212 537 75 41 94/88 18/18 36; Fax : 212 537 75 05 40
E-mail : ambacam@iam.net.com

Canada
EMBASSY : **RABAT**
13 BIS, Rue Jaafar Assedik -Agdal- Rabat
Phone : 212 537 68 74 00; Fax : 212 537 68 74 30
E-mail : rabat@international.gc.ca

Cape-Verde
EMBASSY : Non résident
3, Boulevard Djily Mbaye, Dakar. Senegal.
Phone : 821 18 73 Fax : 821 06 97

Central African Republic
EMBASSY : **RABAT**
65, Rue 29 Youssoufia est-extension de l'etat, BP. 770 Agdal
Phone: 212 537 65 89 70; Fax: 212 537 65 92 16
E-mail: centreafriquemaghreb1@menara.ma

Chad
EMBASSY : Non résident
65, Rue des Belles Feuilles - 75116 Paris - FRANCE
Phone : 00 331 553 36 75 Fax : 00 331 45 53 16 09

Chile
EMBASSY : **RABAT**
35, Avenue Ahmed Balafrej - Souissi - Rabat
Phone : 212 537 63 60 65; Fax : 212 537 63 60 67
Email : echilema@mtds.com

China
EMBASSY : **RABAT**
16, Avenue Ahmed Balafrej, Souissi - Rabat
Phone : 212 537 75 40 56; Fax : 212 537 75 75 19
E-mail : chinaemb-ma.mfa.gov.cn

Colombia
EMBASSY : Non résident
C/O General Martinez Campos 48 - 28010 Madrid, Spain
Phone : 00 34 91 700 4770 Fax : 00 34 91 310 2869

Comoros
EMBASSY : Non résident
4, Rue Said Abdul Wahed- Mohandissine, Cairo, Egypt
Phone : 00 202 347 56 57

Congo (Democratic Republic)
EMBASSY : **RABAT**
34, Avenue de la Victoire- B.P. 553, Rabat-Chellah, Rabat
Phone : 212 537 26 22 80; Fax : 212 537 20 74 07
E-mail : ambardcrabat60@yahoo.fr

Congo (Rep.)
EMBASSY : **RABAT**
AV General Abdenbi Britel OLM 197 Souissi, Rabat
Phone : 212 537 65 99 66; Fax : 212 537 65 99 59

Costa Rica
EMBASSY : Non résident
P° De La Castellana, 164 A 28046 - Madrid, Spain
Phone : 00 91 345 96 22 Fax : 00 91 353 37 09

Cote d'Ivoire
EMBASSY : **RABAT**
7, Rue Ouled Said, B.P 192, Souissi - RABAT
Phone : 212 537 65 57 70; Fax : 212 537 65 56 37
E-mail : ambci_maroc@yahoo.fr

Croatia
EMBASSY : **RABAT**
73, Rue Marnissa - Souissi -Rabat
Phone : 212 537 63 88 24; Fax : 212 537 63 88 27
Email : croemb.rabat@mvpei.hr

Cyprus
EMBASSY : Non resident
AV. DA LIBERDADE 229, LISBON
Phone : 00 35 11 21 31 94 180; Fax : 00 35 11 21 31 97 189

Czech (Rep. Czech)
EMBASSY : **RABAT**
Villa Merzaa, Zankat Ait Melloul, Route des Zaers Souissi
Rabat, B.P. 410
Phone : 00 212 537 75 54 21; Fax : 00212 537 75 43 93
Email : rabat@embassy.mzv.cz Website : www.mfa.cz/rabat

Denmark
EMBASSY : **RABAT**
14, Rue Tiddas angle Rue Roudana, Quartier Hassan, Rabat
Phone : 00 212 537 66 50 20; Fax : 00 212 537 66 50 21
Email : rbaamb@um.dk Website: www.rabat.um.dk

Djibouti
EMBASSY : Non resident
26, Rue Emile Menier 75 116 -PARIS, France
Phone : 00 331 47 274 922 Fax : 00 33 1 45 535 053

Dominican Republic
EMBASSY : Non resident
45 Rue de Courcelles, 75008 Paris, France
Phone : 00 331 53539595 Fax : 00 331 45633563
Email : embajadadom@wanadoo.fr

Ecuador
EMBASSY : Non resident
Via di Posta Angelica N° 63.00193, Rome - Italy

Phone : 066897179 Fax : 0668892786

Egypt
EMBASSY : **RABAT**
31, Av d'Alger Hassan Rabat
Phone : 212 537 73 18 33; Fax : 212 537 70 68 21

El Salvador
EMBASSY : Non resident
C/O General Oraa 9.5 A 28006, Madrid, Spain
Phone: 00 91 562 80 02Fax: 00 91 563 05 84

Equatorial Guinea
EMBASSY : **RABAT**
Villa "SIDNA" AV. le President Roosvelt, 9 Rue d'Agadir, Rabat
Phone : 212 537 66 03 37

Eritrea
EMBASSY : Non resident
6, Rue Al Fallah, Mohandissine, Cairo, Egypt
Phone : 00 202 303 35 03 Fax : 00 202 303 05 16

Estonia
EMBASSY : Non resident
Rua Felipe Folque, N° 10J LISBON, Portugal
Phone : 00 91 426 16 71 Fax : 00 91 426 16 72
Email : embest@embest.pt Website: www.embest.pt

Ethiopia
EMBASSY : Non resident
35, Avenue Charles Floquet 75007 Paris, France
Phone : 00 331 47 83 83 95 Fax : 00 331 43 06 52 14

Finland
EMBASSY : RABAT
145, Rue Soufiance Ben wahb OLM-RABAT,
Phone: 212 537 65 87 75 Fax : 212 537 65 89 04
E-mail : sanomat.rab@formin.fi

France
EMBASSY : RABAT
3, Rue Sahnoun, Agdal, Rabat
Phone : 212 537 68 97 00 Fax : 212 537 68 97 01
Website : www.ambafrance-ma.org
CONSULATE GENERAL : AGADIR
Boulevard Mohamed Cheikh Saadi, Agadir
Phone : 212 528 29 91 50 Fax : 212 528 29 91 51
CONSULATE GENERAL : CASABLANCA
Avenue Prince Moulay abdallah, Casablanca
Phone : 212 522 48 93 00 Fax : 212 522 48 93 05
CONSULATE GENERAL : FES
Avenue Abou Obeida Ibn Al Jarrah,FES, Phone: 212 555 94 94 00
Fax : 212 555 94 94 36
CONSULATE GENERAL : MARRAKECH
Angle Rue Adarissa et El Jahid, HIVERNAGE,BP 538, Marrakech
Phone : 212 544 38 82 00 Fax : 212 544 38 82 33
CONSULATE GENERAL : RABAT
49, AV. Allal Ben Abdallah, BP 139, RABAT
Phone : 212 537 26 91 81 Fax : 212 537 26 91 71
CONSULATE GENERAL : TANGIER
2, Place de France, BP 1281,Tangier
Phone : 212 539 33 96 00 Fax : 212 539 33 96 02

Gabon
EMBASSY : RABAT
Rue Ahmed Rifai N° 52, Souissi, BP 1239, Rabat: Phone : 212 537 75
19 50 Fax : 212 537 75 75 50 E-mail : ambagabon@menara.ma

Gambia
EMBASSY : RABAT
11, Rue Cadi Ben Hammadi Senhadji, Souissi, RABAT
Phone : 212 537 63 80 45 Fax : 212 537 75 29 08

Germany
EMBASSY : RABAT
N° 7, Rue Madnine, B.P. 235, Rabat. Phone : 212 537 70 96 62
Fax : 212 57 70 68 51 Email : amballma@mtds.com

Ghana
EMBASSY : Rabat
27, Rue Ghomara, La Pinede,Souissi, Rabat.
Phone: 212 537 75 76 20 Fax : 212 537 75 76 30
Email : ghanaemb@menara.ma

Greece
EMBASSY : RABAT
Route des Zaers, KM 5, Villa Chems, Souissi, Rabat.
Phone : 212 537 63 89 64 Fax : 212 537 63 89 90
Web page : gremb.rab@mfa.gr

Guinea
EMBASSY : RABAT
15, Rue Hamza - Agdal, Rabat. Phone: 212 537 67 41 48
Fax : 212 537 67 50 70 Email : ambaguirabat@gmail.com

Guinea Bissau
EMBASSY : Non resident
Rue 6, Angle B Point E - Dakar - Senegal
Phone : 00 824 59 22 Fax : 00 824 59 22

Honduras
EMBASSY : Non resident
C/O Paseo de la Castellana,164 2° DCHA - Madrid 28046, Spain
Phone : 00 91 579 02 51 Fax : 91 345 06 65
Email : honduras@tasi.es

Hungary
EMBASSY : RABAT
17, Zankat Aït Melloul, Route des Zaeirs,Souissi, BP 5026, Rabat
Phone : 212 537 75 75 03 Fax : 212 537 75 41 23

Iceland
EMBASSY : Non resident
8, Avenue Kleber- 75116 Paris, France
Phone: 00 331 44 17 32 92 Fax: 00 331 40 67 99 96

India
EMBASSY : RABAT
13, Boulevard Michlifen, Agdal, Rabat. Phone: 212 537 67 1339
Fax : 212 537 67 12 69
Email : india@maghrebnet.net.ma
Website: www.indianembassymorocco.ma

Indonesia
EMBASSY : RABAT
63, Rue Beni Boufrah, KM 5,9, Route des Zaers,Souissi,Rabat
Phone: 212 537 75 78 60 Fax : 212 537 75 78 59
Email : kbri@menara.ma

Iraq
EMBASSY : RABAT
Angle Rue Mehdi Ben Barka et Zankat Mohamed El Ghazi, Souissi
Rabat. Phone : 212 537 75 44 66 Fax : 212 537 75 97 49
Email : rbtemb@iraqmofamail.net

Ireland
EMBASSY : Non resident
Rua Da Imprensa A Estrela, N° 1-4 - 1200 -684 - LISBOA - Portugal
Phone: 351 1 396 94 40 Fax: 351 1 397 73 63 E-mail : lisbon@dfa.ie

Italy
EMBASSY : RABAT
2, Rue Idriss El Azhar, B.P. 111, Rabat. Phone: 212 537 21 97 30
Fax : 212 537 70 68 82. E-mail : ambassade.rabat@esteri.it
CONSULATE GENERAL : CASABLANCA
21, Avenue Hassan Souktani, Casablanca
Phone : 212 522 27 75 58 Fax : 212 522 27 71 39

Japan
 EMBASSY : RABAT
39, Avenue Ahmed Balafrej. Souissi, Rabat
Phone : 212 537 63 17 82
Fax : 212 537 75 00 78

Jordan
EMBASSY : RABAT
65, Villa Wafaa, Logement militaire, Souissi II, Rabat.
Phone: +212 537 75 11 25 Fax : 212 537 75 87 22
Email : jo.am@iam.net.ma

Kazakhstan
EMBASSY : Non resident
73, Charia 15 Sarai El Maadi, Cairo, Egypt
Phone : 00 202 35 98 421 Fax : 00 202 38 09 271
Email : kazaemb@intouch.com

Kenya
EMBASSY : Non résident
29, Rue Al Qods Acharif , Al Mohandissine, Cairo, Egypt.
Phone : 202 345 39 07 Fax : 202 302 69 79

Kuwait
EMBASSY : RABAT
KM 4,300 - Avenue Imam Malik, Souissi, Rabat
Phone : 212 537 63 11 11 Fax : 212 537 75 35 91

Laos
EMBASSY : Non resident
74,venue Rymond - Poincaré, 75116 Paris, France
Phone : 00 33 1 45 53 02 98 Fax : 00 33 1 47 27 57 89

Latvia
EMBASSY : Non resident
N° 17, 2100 Copenhague, Danemark
Phone : 00 45 39 27 60 00 Fax : 00 45 39 27 61 73
E-mail : embassy.denmark@mfa.gov.lv

Lebanon
EMBASSY : RABAT
114, Avenue Abdelmalek Ben Marouane, Rabat
Phone : 212 537 65 69 49 Fax : 212 537 65 71 95

Liberia

EMBASSY : RABAT

23, Rue Qadi Ben Hamadi Senhaji, Souissi, Rabat

Phone : 212 537 63 84 26 Fax : 212 537 63 84 26

Libya

EMBASSY : RABAT

Avenue Imam Malek,KM 5,5, Route Des Zaers, Souissi, Rabat

Phone : 212 537 63 18 71 Fax : 212 537 63 18 77

CONSULATE GENERAL : CASABLANCA

AV. des Far, Imm. Habous, 2e Etage, CASABLANCA

Phone : 212 522 54 15 05 Fax : 212 522 54 15 14

Madagascar

EMBASSY : Non resident

Villa 104, Route de Ouakam, Mermoz Sotrc, Dakar, Senegal

Phone : 00 221 860 29 87 Fax : 00221 860 29 95

Email : ambdak@yahoo.com

Malawi

EMBASSY : Non resident

Gharegharesh, Al Madina Al Syahia Maahad Al Nafta Al Raelsy Street

B.P 83333, Tripoli, Libya

Phone : 00 218 21 4839 119 Fax : 00 218 21 4839 119

Email : malawiembassytripoli@yahoo.com

Malaysia

EMBASSY : RABAT

17, Avenue Bir Kacem, Souissi,Rabat.

Phone: 212 537 65 83 24

Fax : 212 537 65 83 63

Email : mwrabat@menara.ma

Mali

EMBASSY : RABAT

7, Rue Thami Lamdaouar, Souissi, Rabat

Phone : 212 537 75 91 21 Fax : 212 537 75 47 42

Mauritania
EMBASSY : RABAT
6, Rue Thami Lamdaouar, Souissi, Rabat. Phone: 212 537 65 66 78
Fax : 212 537 65 66 80 Email : ambarim-rabat@menara.com
Website : www.ambarimrabat.ma

Mexico
EMBASSY : RABAT
6, Rue Kadi Mohamed Brebri, Souissi, Rabat.
Phone : 212 537 63 19 69 Fax : 212 537 63 19 71

Military Sovereign Order of Malta
EMBASSY : RABAT
12,Rue Ghomara, Souissi - Rabat.
Phone : 00212 537 75 08 97
Fax : 00212 537 75 08 97
Email : ambaosmaltemaroc@yahoo.fr

Moldovia
EMBASSY : Non resident
31-31 1400-1881 Lisbon, Portugal
Phone : 00 351 21 300 90 60 Fax : 00 351 21 300 90 67

Mozambique
EMBASSY : Non resident
24, Avenue Babel Dokki, Cairo, Egypt
Phone: 00 202 760 55 05 Fax: 00 202 748 63 78

Myanmar
EMBASSY : Non resident
24 Rue Mohamed Mazhar, Zamalek, Cairo, Egypt
Phone : 00 202 736 26 44 Fax : 00 202 736 67 93

Nepal
EMBASSY : Non resident
23, Avenue El Hassan- Al Mouhandissine, Cairo, Egypt
Phone : 00 202 760 34 26 Fax : 00 202 337 44 47

Netherlands
EMBASSY : RABAT
40, Rue de Tunis, B.P. 329, Rabat.
Phone : 212 537 21 96 00
Fax : 212 537 21 96 65
Email : nlgovrab@mtds.com
Website: Site de l'Ambassade Royale des Pays-Bas au Maroc

New Zealand
EMBASSY : Non resident
Plaza de la Lealtad, N° 2 - 3°, 28014 Madrid, Spain
Phone : 00 91 523 02 26 Fax : 00 91 523 01 71

Nicaragua
EMBASSY : Non resident
P° de la Castellana 127 1° B 28046 - Madrid, Spain
Phone : 00 91 555 55 10 Fax : 00 91 555 57 37

Niger
EMBASSY : RABAT
Secteur 7, AV. Al Haour, Hay Riad, Rabat
Phone : 212 537 56 62 24 Fax : 212 537 56 62 83

Nigeria
EMBASSY : RABAT
70, Avenue Omar Ibn Al-Khattab,Agdal,Rabat.Phone:212 537 67 1857
Fax : 212 537 67 27 39 Email : nigerianrabat@menara.ma

North Korea
EMBASSY : Non resident
6, Rue Salah Ayoub, Zamalek, Cairo, Egypt
Phone : 202 736 95 32 Fax : 202 735 82 19

Norway
EMBASSY : RABAT
9, Rue de Khenifra, Rabat. Phone : 212 537 76 40 84
Fax : 212 537 76 40 88 Email : emb.rabat@mfa.no

Oman
EMBASSY : RABAT
21, Rue Hamza, Agdal, Rabat
Phone : 212 537 67 37 88 Fax : 212 537 67 45 67

Pakistan
EMBASSY : RABAT
37, AV. Ahmed Balafrej, Souissi, Rabat.Phone: 212 537 63 11 92
Fax : 212 537 63 12 43 Email : pareprabat@iam.net.ma

Palestine
EMBASSY : RABAT
10, Rue Anaba, Rabat
Phone : 212 537 76 98 07 Fax : 212 537 76 71 66

Panama
EMBASSY : Non resident
Avenue Helen Keller, LOT C 1400-197 Lisbon, Portugal
Phone : 00 351 21 364 28 99 Fax : 00 351 21 364 45 89

Paraguay
EMBASSY : Non resident
n° 21 4° IZQDA DA28010 - Madrid, Spain
Phone : 00 91 308 27 46
Fax : 00 91 308 49 05
Email : embapar@arrakis.es

Peru
EMBASSY : RABAT
16, Rue d'Ifrane, RABAT.
Phone : 212 537 72 32 36 Fax : 212 537 70 28 03
Email : leprurabat@menara.com

Philippines
EMBASSY : Non resident
Quartier Al Andalous, KM 7, BP 12508 Tripoli, Libya
Phone : 00 218 21 4833966 Fax : 00 218 21 4836158
Email : tripoli-pe76@lttnet.net

Poland
EMBASSY : RABAT
23, Rue Oqbah, Agdal, B.P. 425, Rabat.Phone : 212 537 77 11 73
Fax : 212 537 77 53 20
Email : apologne@menara.ma
Website: www.rabat.polemb.net

Portugal
EMBASSY : RABAT
5, Rue Thami Lamdaouar, Souissi, Rabat. Phone: 212 537 75 6446
Fax : 212 537 75 64 45
Email : ambassade.portugal@menara.ma

Qatar
EMBASSY : RABAT
4, Boulevard Tarik Ibn Ziad, B.P. 1220, Rabat.
Phone: 212 537 76 56 81 Fax : 212 537 76 57 74/ 212 37 76 39 45

Serbia
EMBASSY : RABAT
23, Rue Mehdi Ben Barka,B.P. 5014m Souiss, Rabat
Phone : 212 537 75 22 01/37 70 Fax : 212 537 75 32 58
Email : sermont@menara.ma

Romania
EMBASSY : RABAT
10, Rue Oouezzane, Rabat. Phone : 212 537 73 86 11
Fax : 212 537 70 01 96
Email : amb.roumanie@menara.ma

Russia
EMBASSY : RABAT
KM 4 - Avenue Imam Malik, Souissi, Rabat. Phone: 212 537 75 36 09
/ 75 35 09 Fax : 212 537 75 35 90 Email : ambrus@iam.net.ma
CASABLANCA
31, Rue Soumaya, Maarif, Casablanca. Phone: 212 522 25 18 73
Fax : 212 522 98 93 57 Email : consul@wanadoo.net.ma

The Vatican
EMBASSY : RABAT
Rue Beni M'tir, B.P. 1303, Souissi, Rabat. Phone : 212 537 77 22 77
Fax : 212 537 75 62 13
Website : nuntius@iam.net.ma

Sao Tome-et-Principe
EMBASSY : Non resident
26 - 1000-017 Lisbon, Portugal
Phone : 00 351 21846 19 17 Fax : 00 351 21846 18 95

Saudi Arabia
EMBASSY : RABAT
322,Av Imam Malik. Km 3.500 Route des Zaers, Rabat
Phone : 212 537 63 30 00 Fax : 212 537 63 96 96

Senegal
EMBASSY : RABAT
Rue Cadi Ben Hamadi Senhaji,Souissi,Rabat. Phone: 212 537 75 4171
Fax : 212 537 75 41 49 E-mail : ambassene@menara.ma
CONSULAT GENERAL : CASABLANCA
20, Rue Ahfir, Anfa, Casablanca. Phone : 212 522 39 00 43
Fax : 212 522 39 00 77 Email : congencas@menara.ma

South Africa
EMBASSY : RABAT
34, Rue Des Saadiens, Hassan, Rabat. Phone: 212 537 70 67 60
Fax : 212 537 70 67 56 Email : sudaf@mtds.com

South Korea
EMBASSY : RABAT
41, Avenue Mehdi Ben Barka, Souissi,Rabat.Phone: 212 537 75 67 91
Fax : 212 537 75 01 89 Email : morocco@mofat.go.kr

Spain
EMBASSY : RABAT
Rue Ain Khalouiya, Rte.des Zaers, Km 5.300 Souissi-Rabat
Phone: 2125 37 63 39 00 Fax: 212 537 63 06 00

Email : emb.rabat@mae.es
CONSULATE GENERAL : CASABLANCA
31, Rue d'Alger, 21000 Casablanca
Phone : 212 522 22 07 52 Fax : 212 522 20 50 49
CONSULATE GENERAL : AGADIR
49,Rue Ibn Batouta Secteur Mixte - BP 3179-80005, Agadir
Phone : 212 548 84 57 10 Fax : 212 548 84 58 43
CONSULATE GENERAL : LARACHE
1, Rue Casablanca, BP:6 (Residence in Tetouan)
Phone : 212 539 91 33 02 Fax : 212 539 91 53 92
CONSULATE GENERAL : NADOR
47 Boulevard Hassan II, BP 7,
Phone : 212 556 60 61 36 Fax : 212 556 60 61 52
CONSULATE GENERAL : RABAT
1, Avenue Ennassr , Rabat
Phone : 212 537 68 74 70 Fax : 212 537 68 18 56
CONSULATE GENERAL : TANGER
85 Avenue Président Habib Bourguiba,Tanger.
Phone : 212 539 93 70 00 Fax : 212 539 93 27 70
CONSULATE GENERAL : TETOUAN
34,Avenue Mohammed V, BP 702, Tetouan
Phone : 212 539 70 39 84 Fax : 212 539 70 44 85

Sudan
EMBASSY : RABAT
5, Rue Ghomara, Souissi - Rabat. Phone : 00 212 537 75 28 63
Fax : 00 212 537 75 28 65 Email : sudanirab@menara.com

Sweden
EMBASSY : RABAT
159, Avenue John Kennedy, BP 428, Souissi, Rabat
Phone: 212 537 63 32 10 Fax : 212 537 75 80 48
Email: ambassade.rabat@foreign.ministry.se
Website: www.swedenabroad.com/rabat

Switzerland
EMBASSY : RABAT
Square de Berkane- 10000, B.P. 169, Rabat

Phone: 212 537 26 80 30 Fax : 212 537 26 80 40
Email : vertretung@rab.rep.admin.ch
Website : www.eda.admin.ch/rabat

Syria
EMBASSY : RABAT
Route des Zaers, KM 5,2, Souissi, Rabat. Phone : 212 537 75 75 21
Fax : 212 37 75 75 22 Email : syriaembassy@menara.ma
Thailand
EMBASSY : RABAT
33, Rue Lalla Meriem, Souissi, Rabat.
Phone : 2125 37 63 46 03 Fax : 212 537 63 46 07
Email : thaima@menara.ma

Tunisia
EMBASSY : RABAT
6, Aveue de Fes et 1, Rue D'Ifrane.
Phone : 212 537 73 06 36 Fax : 212 537 73 06 37
Email : at-rabat@maghreb.net.ma

Turkey
EMBASSY : RABAT
7, AV. Abdelkrim Benjelloune, Rabat.
Phone : 212 537 66 15 22 Fax : 212 537 66 04 76
Email : amb-tur-rabat@iam.net.ma

Ukraine
EMBASSY : RABAT
212, Rue Moaouya Benhoudaig, Souissi II, Rabat
Phone : 212 537 65 78 40 Fax : 212 537 75 46 79
E-mail : emb_ma@mfa.gov.ua
Website : www.mfa.gov.ua/morocco

United Arab Emirates
EMBASSY : RABAT
11, Avenue des Alaouiyines, Hassan, Rabat
Phone: 212 537 70 70 70 Fax : 212 537 72 41 45
Email : emirabat@iam.net.ma

United Kingdom
EMBASSY : RABAT
28, av. SAR Sidi Mohammed , Souissi, Rabat.
Phone : +212 537 63 33 33 Fax : +212 537 75 87 09
Email : britemb@mtds.com Website : www.britain.org.ma
CONSULATE GENERAL : CASABLANCA
36, Rue de la Loire, Polo, Casablanca. Phone: 212 522 85 74 00
Fax : 212 522 83 46 25 E-mail : british.consulate@menara.ma
CONSULATE : TANGER
9 Rue Amerique du Sud, BP 1203, 90000 Tangier
Phone : 212 539 93 69 39 Fax : 212 539 93 68 14

United States of America
EMBASSY : RABAT
2, Avenue Marrakech, Rabat.
Phone : 212 537 76 22 65 Website: www.usembassy.ma
CONSULATE GENERAL : CASABLANCA
8, Boulevard Moulay Youssef, Casablanca
Phone : 212 522 26 45 50 Email : nivcasablanca@state.gov

Vanuatu
EMBASSY : RABAT
14, Rue El Quiraouane Hassan - Rabat -
Phone : 00 212 537 20 23 73 Fax : 00 212 537 20 23 49

Vietnam
EMBASSY : RABAT
27, Rue Mezzouda, Souissi, Rabat
Phone : 212 537 65 92 56 Fax : 212 537 65 92 10
Email : vnambassade@yahoo.com.vn

Yemen
EMBASSY : RABAT
Charia Imam Malek, Km 6.6, Rue Beni Tajit, Quartier des
Ambassadeurs, Souissi, Rabat. Phone : 212 537 63 12 20
Fax : 212 537 63 12 67 Email : yemen@menara.ma

UNITED NATIONS REPRESENTATIONS

United Nations Development Program - UNDP
Angle Aenue Moulay Hassan et Rue de Safi, Casier ONU – Rabat –
Chellah Phone: 212 537 70 35 55 Fax: 212 537 70 15 66

United Nations Population Fund
Angle avenue Moulay Hassan et Rue de Safi, Casier ONU – Rabat –
Chellah. Phone: 212 537 70 17 58 Fax: 212 537 70 14 82
Email: Mostapha.benzine@undp.org

UN World Food Program
Angle avenue Moulay Hassan et rue de Safi, Casier ONU, Rabat
Phone: 212 537 76 69 82 Fax: 212 537 76 53 66

UN Information Centre - UNIC
6, rue Tarik Ibn Ziad (angle Rue Roudana) Quartier de la Residence,
BP 6001,Rabat, Phone: 212 537 76 86 33 Fax: 212 537 76 83 77

Food and Agriculture Organization of the United Nations - FAO
9, Rue Tiddas,BP 1369,Rabat
Phone: 212 537 76 57 56 Fax: 212 537 76 64 68

The United Nations Children's Fund – UNICEF
28, Rue Oum Rabia – Agdal – Rabat Phone: 212 537 77 22 12
Fax: 212 537 77 24 36

World Health Organisation – WHO
Ministere de la Sante Publique – B.P. 812 Rabat – Mechouar
Phone: 212 537 76 67 44 Fax: 212 537 76 68 05

International Committee of the Red Cross – ICRC
Mr. Werner Caspar (Tunisia)

Offices of the United Nations High Commissioner for Refugees (UNHCR)
13, Rue Blida – B.P. 13434 – Casablanca-Principale Phone: 212 522
20 03 96 Fax: 212 522 27 98 55

UNESCO (United Nations Educationational and Scientific Organisation) representation in Morocco, Algeria and Mauritania
35, Avenue du 16 Novembre – B.P. 1777, R.P, Agdal, Rabat
Phone: 212 537 67 03 74 Fax: 212 537 67 03 75
Email: uhrab@unesco.org

Resident Mission of the World Bank
7, Rue Larbi Ben Adbellah – Souissi – Rabat
Phone: 212 537 63 60 48 Fax: 212 538 63 60 51

International Finance Corporation – IFC
8, Rue Kamal Mohamed – 2eme etage – 20000 Casablanca Phone: 212 522 48 46 86 Fax: 212 522 48 46 90

AFRICAN INSTITUTIONS

Economic Commission for Africa – ECA, Sub-regional Office
Pavillion International – Avenue Mohammed V – B.P. 316 – Tanger
Phone: 212 539 32 23 46 Fax: 212 539 43 03 57

African Training and Research Centre in Administration for Development – CAFRAD
B.P. 310 ,Tangier. Phone: 212 539 94 26 91 Fax: 212 5.39 94 14 15

Association of African Organisations for Trade Promotion-AOAPC
Avenue Mohamed V – Pavillon International 3eme Etage – B.P. 23, Tangier. Phone: 212 539 94 15 36

African Development Bank - ADB
9, Avenue de Tripoli – B.P. 1459 R.P. – Rabat Phone: 212 537 73 05 18 Fax: 212 537 7305 31

Union of North-African Ports (union des administrations portuaires du nord de l'Afrique – uapna)
Secteur 21, Villa M10 – Rue Dadi – Hay Riad – B.P. 2062 – Rabat
Phone: 212 537 71 02 47 Fax: 212 537 71 02 47

INTERNATIONAL FOUNDATIONS

Friedrich Naumann Foundation – FFN
35, Rue Melouya – Agdal – Rabat
Phone: 212 537 77 75 09
Fax: 212 537 77 75 36

Friedrich Ebert Foundation – FFE
2, Rue Tiznit – B.P. 1769 – Rabat
Phone: 212 537 76 28 58 Fax: 212 537 76 98 91

Hanns Siedel Foundation
Rue Cadi Moreno,Souissi, Rabat
Phone: 212 537 75 67 50
Fax: 212 537 75 88 17

Konrad Adenauer Foundation
10, Rue Cadi Abdallah Kabbaj – Souissi – Rabat
Phone: 00 212 537 75 95 85

King Abdulaziz Al Saoud Foundation for Islamic studies and Human Sciences
Boulevard de la Corniche – Ain Diab – B.P. 12585 – Casablanca
Phone: 212 522 39 10 27
Fax: 212 522 39 10 31

Euro-Maghreb Network for Training in Communications skills – REMFOC
77, Avenue Moulay Ismail – Rabat
Phone: 212 537 70 65 91
Fax: 212 537 70 65 91